Samir Amin

Samir Amin has a worldwide reputation as one of the world's foremost radical thinkers. Among his many institutional roles, he has been Director of IDEP (the United Nations African Institute for Planning) from 1970 to 1980; Director of the Third World Forum in Dakar, Senegal; and a co-founder of the World Forum for Alternatives. His recent works published by Zed Books in English include *Eurocentrism* (1989), *Capitalism in the Age of Globalization: The Management of Contemporary Society* (1997) and *Obsolescent Capitalism: Contemporary Politics and Global Disorder* (2003)

Ali El Kenz

Ali El Kenz is Professor of Sociology, Nantes University, France. His work is focused on Arab research in the social sciences and he has published extensively in both French and Arabic.

SAMIR AMIN | ALI EL KENZ

Europe and the Arab world

Patterns and prospects for the new relationship

Zed Books

LONDON | NEW YORK

Europe and the Arab world: Patterns and prospects for the new relationship was first published by Zed Books Ltd, 7 Cynthia Street, London N1 9JF, UK and Room 400, 175 Fifth Avenue, New York, NY 10010, USA in 2005

www.zedbooks.co.uk

First published in Lebanon, Bahrain, Egypt, Jordan, Kuwait, Qatar, Saudi Arabia and United Arab Emirates by World Book Publishing, 282 Emile Eddeh Street, Ben Salem bldg, PO Box 3176, Beirut, Lebanon

Cover designed by Andrew Corbett
Set in Dante and Gill Sans Heavy by Ewan Smith, London
Index: ed.emery@britishlibrary.net
Printed and bound in the UK by Biddles Ltd, King's Lynn

Distributed in the USA exclusively by Palgrave Macmillan, a division of St Martin's Press, LLC, 175 Fifth Avenue, New York, NY 10010.

A catalogue record for this book is available from the British Library.
US CIP data are available from the Library of Congress.

ISBN 9953 14 068 5 pb: Lebanon
ISBN 1 84277 436 0 hb: rest of the world
ISBN 1 84277 437 9 pb

Contents

Acknowledgements

This book identifies the ambiguities and the limitations of the social movements and struggles within the Arab world. In that frame the patterns and prospects for the new relationship between Europe and the Arab world are assessed.

Chapters 1, 2 and 4 have been written by Samir Amin and Chapter 3 by Ali El Kenz.

The views expressed here were the subject of a debate organized in Cairo by Third World Forum, the World Forum for Alternatives and the Arab Research Centre. This debate benefited from the support of the Rosa Luxemburg Stiftung (Berlin), the Norwegian agency for international cooperation Norad, Novib in the Netherlands, and Luxembourg's agency for international cooperation. The opinions expressed in this book are those of their authors alone.

1 | The Arab world: a balance sheet of the present situation and struggles

What follows is an attempt to identify the questions posed by movements and struggles within the Arab world, analysing and assessing their ambiguities and limitations. It takes the inherent contradictions of the system as a starting point, identifying the conditions for popular and democratic progress that might be facilitated by these struggles.

The autocratic state faced with the challenge of modernity

There is no democratic state in the Arab world. There are only autocratic states. Although autocratic, Arab political regimes have not always been – and still are not – without legitimacy in the eyes of their own societies. According to Hashem Sharaby, state power has always been synonymous with personal power, as opposed to the power of the law defining the modern state. This Weber-like descriptive analysis is worth qualifying since the personal (or personalized) powers in question are legitimate only in so far as they are proclaimed as being respectful of the tradition (and especially of the religious *shariah*) and are perceived as such. From a more in-depth perspective, Sharaby establishes a relationship between autocracy and the 'patriarchal' nature of the system of social values. The term 'patriarchy' is understood here to be more than what is ascribed to the popularized commonplace term of 'male chauvinism' (asserting and practising the marginalization of women in society). The patriarchy in question is a system that upholds the duty of obedience at all levels: school and family education nip in the bud the slightest hint of criticism and hierarchies are sacrosanct in the family system (subordinating women and children), in the business sector (subordinating the employee to the employer), in public service (demanding absolute submission to superiors), in the absolute prohibition of unorthodox religious interpretation, etc. This observation links up with the conclusions that I have drawn from the definition of modernity and from the challenge it constitutes.

Modernity is based on the principle that human beings create their history individually and collectively and that, to that extent, they have the right to innovate and to disregard tradition. Proclaiming this principle meant breaking with the fundamental principle that governed all pre-modern societies, including of course those of feudal and Christian Europe. Modernity was born with this proclamation. It had nothing to do with rebirth; it was simply a question of birth. The tag 'Renaissance' that Europeans themselves gave to history in this era is therefore misleading. It is the result of an ideological construction purporting that Graeco-Roman antiquity was acquainted with the principle of modernity, which was veiled in the 'Middle Ages' (between the old modernity and the new modernity) by religious obscurantism. It was the mythical perception of antiquity that in turn paved the way for Eurocentrism, whereby Europe claims to go back to its past, 'to return to its sources' (hence, the Renaissance), whereas in fact, it is engineering a break with its own history. The European Renaissance was the product of an internal social process, the solution found to contradictions peculiar to the then Europe through the invention of capitalism. On the other hand, what the Arabs by imitation referred to as their Renaissance – the *nahda* of the nineteenth century – was not one either. It was the reaction to an external shock. The Europe that modernity had rendered powerful and triumphant had an ambiguous effect on the Arab world through attraction (admiration) and repulsion (through the arrogance of its conquest). The Arab Renaissance takes its qualifying term literally. It is assumed that, if the Arabs 'returned' to their sources, as the Europeans claim to have done, they would regain their greatness, even if debased for some time. The *nahda* does not know the nature of the modernity that enhances Europe's power.

This is not the place to refer to different aspects and moments marking *nahda*'s deployment. I will just state briefly that *nahda* does not forge the necessary break with tradition that defines modernity. Nahda does not recognize the meaning of secularism, in other words, separation between religion and politics, the condition that ensures that politics serves as the field for free innovation, and for that matter, for democracy in the modern sense. *Nahda* thinks it can substitute for secularism an interpretation of religion purged of its obscurantist drifts. At any rate, to date, Arab societies are not adequately equipped to understand that secularism is not a 'specific' characteristic of the

Western world but rather a requirement for modernity. *Nahda* does not realize the meaning of democracy, which should be understood as the right to break with tradition. It therefore remains captive to the concepts of the autocratic state; it hopes and prays for a 'just' despot (*al moustabid al adel*) – even if not 'enlightened', and the nuance is significant. *Nahda* does not understand that modernity also promotes women's aspirations to freedom, thereby exercising their right to innovate and break with tradition. Eventually, *nahda* reduces modernity to the immediate aspect of what it produces: technical progress. This voluntarily over-simplified presentation does not mean that I am not aware of the contradictions expressed in *nahda*, nor that certain avant-garde thinkers were aware of the real challenges posed by modernity, such as Kassem Amin and the importance of women's emancipation, Ali Abdel Razek and secularism, and Kawakibi and the challenge posed by democracy. However, none of these breakthroughs had any effect; on the contrary, Arab society reacted by refusing to follow the paths indicated. *Nahda* is therefore not the time marking the birth of modernity in the Arab world but rather the period of its abortion.

Since the Arab states have not yet embraced modernity, Arabs still accept to a large extent these principles of autocratic power, which maintains its legitimacy or loses it in fields other than its non-recognition of the principle of democracy. If it is able to resist imperialist aggression – or to give that impression – if it is able to promote a visible improvement of the material living conditions of many, if not all, autocratic power enjoys guaranteed popularity. Beyond this non-modernity principle, autocratic power therefore owes its legitimacy to tradition. In some cases, this could refer to a tradition of national and religious monarchy such as that of Morocco or of a tribal monarchy in the Arabian peninsula. But there is another form of tradition – the one inherited from the Ottoman Empire, dominant in the territory between Algeria and Iraq, and therefore influencing the largest segment of the Arab world – which I describe as the tradition of 'mameluke power'. This is about a complex system that associated the personalized power of warlords, businessmen and men of religion. I emphasize men, since women are obviously not allowed to assume any responsibilities. The three dimensions of this organization are not merely juxtaposed; they are actually merged into a single reality of power.

The mamelukes are men of war who owe their legitimacy to a certain concept of Islam that places emphasis on the opposite of *Dar El Islam* (the Muslim world – a community governed by the rules of peaceful management)/*Dar El Harb* (extra-Muslim world, the place for the pursuit of *jihad*, 'Holy War'). It is not by chance that this military concept of political management was fabricated by the conquering Seljuk Turks and the Ottomans, who called themselves 'Ghazi' – conquerors and colonizers of Byzantine Anatolia. It is not by chance that the mamelukes' system was built from the era of Salah El Dine, liberator of the Holy Lands occupied until then by the Crusaders. Populist powers and contemporary nationalists always mention the name of Salah El Dine with respectful admiration without ever considering or making any allusion to the ravages of the system from which it originated. At the end of the Crusades, the Arab world (which became Turkish-Arab) entered into a military feudalization and isolation process reflecting a decline that put an end to the brilliant civilization of the early centuries of the Caliphate while Europe was beginning to discard feudalism and preparing to embark on the invention of modernity and move on to conquer the world. In compensation for this service as protectors of Islam, the mamelukes gave the men of religion a monopoly in the interpretation of dogmas, of justice rendered in the name of Islam and in the moral civilization of the society. Relegated to its purely traditional social dimension – respect for rites being the sole important consideration – religion is absolutely subjugated by the autocratic power of men of war. Economic life is then subject to the mood of the military-political authority. Whenever possible, the peasantry is directly subjected to the whims of this ruling class and private property is jeopardized (the related principle being indisputably sacralized by the fundamental texts of Islam). The proceeds of trade are also sequestered.

The mameluke ruling class naturally aspired to the dispersion of its autocratic power. Formally responsible to the Sultan-Caliph, the mamelukes took advantage of the long distance then separating them from the capital (Istanbul) to personally exercise full powers within the radius of the land under their control. In areas with an age-old tradition of state centralization, such as Egypt, there have been successive attempts to discipline the whole military corps. It is not by chance that Mohamed Ali established his centralized authority by massacring the mamelukes, but only to re-establish a military–real estate aristocracy under his personal authority from that time onwards. The Beys of Tunis tried to do likewise on a more modest scale. The Deys of Algiers never succeeded in doing so. The Ottoman Sultanate did so in turn, thereby integrating its Turkish, Kurdish and Armenian provinces of Anatolia and its Arab provinces of historic Syria and Iraq under an authority 'modernized' that way. Just modernization? Or just a modernized autocracy? Enlightened despotism? Or just despotism? The fluctuations and variants are situated in this range, which does not usher in anything making it possible to go beyond it. Certainly, the typical autocratic model of mameluke had to reckon with the numerous and diverse realities that always defined the real limits. Peasant communities that took refuge in their fortified mountains (Kabylians, Maronites, Druzeans, Alawites, etc.), Sufi brotherhoods almost everywhere and tribes obliged the dominant authorities to reach a compromise with and tolerate rebellious groups. The contrast in Morocco between Maghzen and Bled Siba is of a similar nature.

Have the forms in which power was exercised in the Arab world changed so much as to justify the assertion that those described here belong to a distant past? The autocratic state and the related forms of political management certainly exist to date. However, they are beset with a profound crisis that has already curtailed their legitimacy, as they were increasingly incapable of meeting the challenges posed by modernity.

Political Islam

It would be a fatal error to assume that the emergence of mass political movements identified with Islam is the inevitable outcome of the rise of a culturally and politically backward people who cannot understand any language other than that of their quasi-atavistic obscurantism. Muslims and Islam have a history, just like that of the other regions of the world. It is a history fraught with diverse interpretations concerning linkages between reason and faith, a history of mutual transformation and adaptation of both society and its religion. However, the reality of this history is denied not only by Eurocentric discourses but also by the contemporary movements associated with Islam. In fact, the two entities have the same cultural bias whereby the 'specific' features ascribed to the different careers of their own peoples and religions are allegedly intangible, infinite and transhistorical. To the Western world's Eurocentrism, contemporary political Islam opposes solely an inverted Eurocentrism.

The emergence of movements claiming to be Islamic is actually expressive of a violent revolt against the destructive effects of actually existing capitalism and against its attendant unaccomplished, truncated and deceptive modernity. It is an expression of an absolutely legitimate revolt against a system that has nothing to offer to the peoples concerned. The discourse of the Islam proposed as an alternative to capitalist modernity (to which the modern experiences of historical socialisms are clearly assimilated) is political by nature. The heralds of the said 'Islamic Renaissance' are not interested in theology. Hence, what they understand by Islam appears to be solely a conventional and social version of religion limited to the formal and integral respect for ritual practice. The Islam in question would define a community to which one belongs by inheritance, like ethnicity instead of a strong and intimate personal conviction. It is solely a question of asserting a 'collective identity' and nothing more. This is the reason why the term 'political Islam' –instead of 'fundamentalism' – is certainly more appropriate to qualify all these movements in Arab countries. The proposed Islam is in this case the adversary of every liberation theology. Political Islam advocates submission and not emancipation. It was only Mahmoud Taha of Sudan who attempted to emphasize the element of emancipation in his interpretation of Islam. Sentenced to death and executed by the authorities of Khartoum, Taha was not acknowledged by any 'radical' or 'moderate' Islamic group, and neither was he defended by any of the intellectuals identifying themselves with 'Islamic Renaissance' or even by those who are merely willing to 'dialogue' with such movements.

Modern political Islam had been invented by the orientalists in the service of the British authority in India before being adopted intact by Mawdudi of Pakistan. It consisted in 'proving' that Muslim believers are not allowed to live in a state that is itself not Islamic – anticipating the partition of India – because Islam would ignore the possibility of separation between state and religion. The orientalists in question failed to observe that the English of the thirteenth century would not have conceived of their survival either without Christianity! Abul Ala Al Mawdudi therefore took up the theme, stipulating that power comes from God alone (*wilaya al faqih*), thus repudiating the concept of citizens having the right to make laws, the state being solely entrusted with enforcement of the law defined once and for all (the *shariah*). Joseph de Maistre had already written similar things, accusing the French Revolution of inventing modern democracy and individual emancipation. Refuting the concept of emancipatory modernity, political Islam disapproves of the very principle of democracy – the right of society to build its own future through its freedom to legislate. The *shura* principle is not the Islamic form of democracy, as claimed by political Islam, for it is hampered by the ban on innovation (*ibda*), and accepts, if need be, only that of interpretation of the tradition (*ijtihad*). The *shura* is only one of the multiple forms of the consultation found in all pre-modern and pre-democratic societies. Of course, interpretation has sometimes been the vehicle for real changes imposed by new demands. However, the fact remains that by virtue of its own principle – denial of the right to break with the past – interpretation leads into deadlock the modern fight for social change and democracy. The parallel claimed between the Islamic parties – radical or moderate, since all of them adhere to the same 'anti-modernist' principles in the name of the so-called specificity of Islam – and Christian Democrat parties of modern Europe is therefore not valid, strictly speaking, even though American media and diplomatic circles continue to make allusions to the said parallel so as to legitimize their support of possibly 'Islamist' regimes. Christian Democracy is an element of modernity of which it upholds the fundamental concept of creative democracy as the essential aspect of the concept of secularism. Political Islam refuses modernity and proclaims this fact without being able to understand its significance. Moreover, these movements' discourse solely reflects Wahabite Islam, which rejects all that the interaction between historical Islam and Greek philosophy had produced in its epoch, as it merely turned over the unimaginative writings of Ibn Taymiya, the most reactionary of the theologians of the Middle Ages. Although some of his heralds qualify this interpretation as 'a return to the sources', it is actually a mere reference to the notions that prevailed two hundred years ago, notions of a society whose development has been stalled for several centuries.

Contemporary political Islam is not the outcome of a reaction to the so-called abuses of secularism, as often claimed, unfortunately. It is because no Muslim society of modern times – except in the former Soviet Union – has ever been truly secular, let alone appalled at the daring innovations of any atheistic and aggressive power. The semi-modern state of Kemal's Turkey, Nasser's Egypt, Baathist Syria and Iraq merely subjugated the men of religion (as often happened in former times) to impose on them concepts solely aimed at legitimizing their political options. The beginnings of a secular idea existed only in certain critical intellectual circles. In Egypt the secular idea did not have much impact on the state, which sometimes retreated in this respect when obsessed with its nationalist project, thereby causing a break with the policy adopted by the Wafd since 1919, as demonstrated by the disturbing evolution inaugurated even at the time of Nasser. Political Islam intends to perfect an evolution already well established in the countries concerned and aimed at restoring a plainly conservative theocratic order associated with a political power of the 'mameluke' type.

From this fundamental point of view, there is no difference between the so-called 'radical' movements of political Islam and those that wanted to appear 'moderate' because the aims of both entities are identical. The case of Iran itself is not an exception to the general rule, despite the confusions that contributed to its success: the concomitance between the rapid development of the Islamist movement and the struggle waged against the Shah who was socially reactionary and politically pro-American. Political Islam is in fact nothing other than an adaptation to the subordinate status of the comprador capitalism. Its so-called 'moderate' form therefore probably constitutes the principal danger threatening the peoples concerned since the violence of the 'radicals' serves only to destabilize the state to allow for the installation of a new comprador power. The constant support offered by the pro-American diplomacies of the Triad countries towards finding this 'solution' to the problem is absolutely consistent with their desire to impose the globalized liberal order in the service of dominant capital.

The two discourses of globalized liberal capitalism and political Islam do not conflict; they are, rather, complementary. The ideology of American 'communitarianisms' being popularized by current fashion overshadows the conscience and social struggles and substitutes for them so-called collective 'identities' that ignore them. This ideology is therefore perfectly manipulated in the strategy of capital domination because it transfers the struggle from the arena of real social contradictions to the imaginary world that is said to be cultural, transhistorical and absolute, whereas political Islam is precisely a communitarianism. The diplomacy of the G7 powers, and particularly that of the United States, knows what it does in choosing to support political Islam. It has done so in Afghanistan by describing its Islamists as 'freedom fighters' (!) against the horrible dictatorship of 'communism', which was in fact an enlightened, modernist, national and populist despotism that had the audacity to open schools for girls! They continue to do so from Egypt to Algeria. They know that the power of political Islam has the virtue – to them – of making the peoples concerned helpless and consequently ensuring their compradorization without difficulty. Given its inherent cynicism, the American establishment knows how to take a second advantage of political Islam. The 'drifts' of the regimes that it inspires – the Taliban for instance – who do not drift in any way but actually come within the logic of their programmes, can be exploited whenever imperialism finds it expedient to intervene brutally. The 'savagery' attributed to the peoples who are the first victims of political Islam is likely to encourage 'islamophobia' and that facilitates the acceptance of the perspective of a 'global apartheid' – the logical and necessary outcome of an ever-polarizing capitalist expansion. The sole political movements using the label of Islam, which are categorically condemned by the G7 powers, are those involved in anti-imperialist struggles – under the objective circumstances at the local level: Hezbollah in Lebanon and Hamas in Palestine. This is not a matter of chance.

Political conflicts snd social struggles

A quick look at the global situation today would easily reveal that the mameluke power is still in existence.

The first striking similarity with the past consists in the supreme authority exercised by the military institution in Algeria, Egypt, Syria and Iraq; in some areas, the institution is disciplined and strictly subjected to a respected hierarchy (Egypt) while elsewhere, it is parcelled between many generals permanently engaged in muffled or open contentious rivalry (Algeria). Certainly, the military institution is probably not the firm guarantor of stability that it appears to be. At least, even if the military institution is partly influenced by political Islam, and is by no means immunized against the centrifugal forces that can be fanned by ethnic or religious diversity, the fact remains that this institution was the sole inheritor of the populist nationalism that spanned the 1950s, 1960s and 1970s. No doubt, in Morocco, Saudi Arabia and the Gulf Emirates, it is the monarchical institution, which is itself merged with the Moroccan and Wahabite type of religious institution, that directly sees to the transfer of supreme power.

The second striking similarity with the mameluke autocracy lies in the interpenetration of the business world and the world of power. It is because, truly speaking, there is no genuine 'private sector' and not many autonomous capitalists managing their businesses are assured of the ownership of their enterprises. Whenever an authentic private sector exists, it is composed of medium-scale enterprises jostled by the economic situation and liberal globalization. On the other hand, most of the profits accruing from the so-called private economy in the Arab world of the last twenty years appear as real political 'rent'.

The third similarity consists in the exploitation of the traditional conservative religious legitimacy. The more the mameluke–comprador power is compromised by its concrete submission to the dominant imperialist interests, the more it aligns itself with the exigencies of liberal globalization and the more it tries to compensate for the loss of national legitimacy due to such submission which stiffens its so-called 'religious' discourse, thereby generating competition with the rival Islamist movement. That was exactly what the Ottoman and mameluke ancestors did as they yielded to the imperialist diktats of previous centuries!

In any case, in the Arab world, this contemporary resurrection of mameluke autocracy could not have been imagined a century or even fifty years ago. On the contrary, the page seemed to have been turned for good.

In the first phase, the Arab world – at least its Egyptian and Syrian centres – appeared to have embarked on an authentic bourgeois modernization process. Mohamed Ali and then the *nahda* of the nineteenth century seemed to have prepared for this. The Egyptian Revolution of 1919 manifested the first strong expression of the process. It was not by chance that this revolution took place under the closest approximation of secularism known in the history of the Arab world, with the proclamation of 'Religion is for God, the fatherland for all', and the choice of a flag featuring crescent and cross. In the Ottoman Empire, the Tanzimat initiated a parallel evolution inherited by the Arab provinces and which they even developed after the empire's decline. Constitutions, civil codes, 'liberal' bourgeois parties and parliamentary elections inspired the hope that society would move in the right direction despite all its inherent weaknesses and inadequacies. In terms of real economic and social development – which easily found expression in the weakness of the local bourgeoisie *vis-à-vis* the then imperialists and their local reactionary allies, and the aggravation of the social crisis for that matter – the meagre results ultimately ended this first period of ineffective modernization of the Arab world.

The second phase was that of the populist nationalism of the 1950s, 1960s and 1970s. The triumphant Nasserism, Baathism and the Algerian Revolution seemed capable of stemming the social crisis through the deployment of a more determined anti-imperialist policy (promoted with Soviet support) and active economic and social development policies. This page is turned, for reasons which include the system's internal contradictions and restrictions and the reversal of the global economic and political situations. At this time the pre-modern autocratic state resurfaced while society was no longer comparable in any way to the one that had existed a century or even a half-century previously. The social crisis today is incomparably more acute. It is not that society is 'poorer' on the whole. On the contrary, the progression is indisputable in terms of average real income. On the other hand, the key reality concerning changes in this domain consists in the expansion of the middle classes. For instance, in Egypt the upper group of the middle classes increased from 5 per cent to 15 per cent of the country's population in fifty years and the proportion of the middle classes as a whole from 10 per cent to 30 per cent (according to Galal Amin). At any rate, the modernization in question has also been that of poverty. The intensity of the crisis is commensurate with the urbanization of the Arab world, which constitutes its key indicator. More than half of the Arab population is now urbanized. However, this massive transfer is not the outcome of a two-sided agricultural and industrial revolution, more or less similar to the one that built the developed capitalist West or the Soviet world and which contemporary China has embraced for half a century. It is rather the result of the absence of both agricultural revolution and industrial revolution. Growing rural misery is simply transferred to urban areas that modern industries and activities cannot absorb. The structure of social classes and categories in which this crisis found expression no longer has anything to do with that of the Arab world a century or fifty years ago. The page of populist nationalism turned, the discredited single-party system gave way to the explosion of the multi-party system, which the world media hastened to acknowledge as the beginning of a democratic development, naturally and obviously promoted by the opening of markets, as envisaged by the vulgate in fashion. The paradox here is that this explosion of the multi-party system was accompanied by a prodigious regression to the mameluke type of autocracy.

Egypt Nasserism had 'nationalized politics' (actually placed politics under state control) as purported in Egypt; that is, it had used violent repression to suppress the two poles between which the active political forces and public opinion were divided – the bourgeois liberal pole and the communist pole. By this means too was created an ideological vacuum that Islam had to fill gradually in the Nasserian era, and violently from 1970. The influence of the religious institution, encouraged by Nasser's modernization of Al Azhar, did penetrate the expanding middle classes, key beneficiaries of the populism that dawned with improved education and employment. Apparently domesticated, Al Azhar did not manifest any disturbing signs to the regime; that was the time when its *fatwa* justified 'socialism'. The Muslim Brothers, who for some time thought of imposing their presence in the regime, opposed a repression that always proved to be wavering in their regard, as many Free Officers had been closely associated with them. Whereas they were formally dissolved, these entities continued to be tolerated through the 'religious associations' that progressively infiltrated the state machinery, particularly the education, legal and media sectors. When Sadat decided to turn to the right after Nasser's death in 1970, the stage was set to place political Islam abruptly in the limelight with the support of Gulf oil money and American diplomacy. The price lay in the 'opening' (*infitah*) initiated by Nasser after the 1967 defeat, that prepared the ground for reintegration into the global capitalist system, the break with the Soviet alliance and finally the trip to Jerusalem (1977) and subsequently the Madrid/Oslo process (1993). All the same, it still took ten years for the law to establish (in 1979) a 'granted' multi-party system initially limited to the three 'tribunes' of the defunct so-called Socialist Union of the left, centre and right. The unchanged constitution vests the president with powers that place him above the legislature, the executive and the judiciary. The new democracy, granted and controlled ('elections' must guarantee the perpetuation of the power of the president approved by the military institution), was negotiated with the United States, which gave the president its blessing (as per the 1991 agreement between the Government of Egypt and USAID), thereby making it possible for Washington to issue a certificate of democracy to the Egyptian government.

One cannot therefore have illusions about the 'political parties' arising from such combinations. The Democratic National Union does not have a higher profile than the Socialist Union, which it inherited. The latter did not even enjoy the historic legitimacy of the communist party models (of the USSR, China or Vietnam) of which it constituted a caricature. Before enduring the deteriorating effect of their solitary exercise of power, the communist parties in question organized real revolutions. In contrast, the Egyptian Socialist Union was never anything but a collection of opportunists without much conviction, which was convenient for the enlightened despot. The self-dissolution of the Egyptian communist organization in 1965, which was obtained not without reluctance on the part of many militants, did not bring about any considerable improvement in the system, since the government had taken rigorous measures to forestall the materialization of this 'threat' (to it). Among the new political parties, Tagammu, which tried to rally the Nasserian leftists, and inheritors of Egyptian communism, suffered the defection of the Nasserians. Nostalgic for the past, and apparently lacking the capacity to understand the nature of the new challenges, the old Nasserians contented themselves with the rhetoric of the Arab nationalist discourse (*qawmi*) and therefore initiated a process of reconciliation with the Islamists, who were also fond of simple rhetoric. At any rate, Tagammu will remain a hope for the revival of a political debate worthy of its name, provided it succeeds in mobilizing the militant traditions it has so far been trying to benumb. The Labour Party organized by Adel Hussein (died in 2001) had to mobilize the Islamist discourse with greater apprehension, in presenting himself as the rival to the traditional leaders of the Muslim Brotherhoods.

Hitherto, the Egyptian parties' political democracy therefore did not go beyond a bottled-up campaign. Renouncing any form of action – which the regime formally prohibited – and contenting themselves with discourses, these parties did not present themselves as a real alternative to the ruling power. They did not develop credible alternative programmes but rather took to criticizing government action intermittently.

The resultant drift occasioned by this political vacuum did contribute to the reaffirmation of the mameluke autocratic tradition. The most disturbing demonstration of this drift unexpectedly found expression during the last parliamentary elections (1999): a crowd of so-called 'independent' candidates exploited the possibilities that this situation offered to them. They were not opponents, even disguised, but rather candidates for this class of 'entrepreneurs – fundholders supported by the state' (typical of the mameluke system) who often managed to form a group of lobbyists sufficient to 'win' the election amid the indifference of the majority of the population. The liberal 'academics' – Americans among others – who hailed the expression 'birth of a bourgeoisie of entrepreneurs' probably misled ignorant external opinion, not the Egyptian people. Under these circumstances, the sole force that presents itself as an alternative to the real power – that of the military institution – is represented by the Muslim Brotherhood. However, the latter have no other project than that of an autocratic power of the same nature, in which the religious institution would take the place of that of the military. As for the rest – adhering to the globalized liberalism and local money-oriented comprador economy – there is no difference. That is the reason why the diplomacy of Washington actually sees in them an alternative solution, if necessary.

Nasser's regime was the planned project of an enlightened despot. The regime's socio-economic project was a real one implemented with determination. This is why, in spite of its dictatorial and police behaviour, the regime had to take – and did take – into account the social forces which expressed themselves through workers' unions, student movements, professional associations, rural cooperatives, the media and intellectuals. Moreover, Nasser's political language had a name for these agencies – *marakez quwa* (power centres) – and this testified to the acknowledgement of the fact.

In Egypt, there are 25,000 union committees (which still exist) integrated into twenty-three unions that formed a single confederation of trade unions (General Workers' Union of Egypt) during Nasser's regime. This body rallied between 3 and 4 million real members (probably small, in comparison with the 15 to 17 million wage earners, but already considerable, as the number included almost all the salaried employees of modern enterprises). Nasserism had given them real powers, not to participate in the running of enterprises (these powers were a mere façade) but rather to manage workforce and living conditions (housing, consumer cooperatives, etc.). Having renounced 'class struggles', the working class was compensated with improved material living conditions. However, the militant spirit and communist influence continued to exist at the grassroots (in the 25,000 local committees) even though the regime took steps to gain effective control over the unions by appointing loyal agents to managerial positions at national level. This explains the low permeability of the working class that hitherto clamoured for political Islam.

What is the situation today? First, the emigration, openly promoted as from 1970, certainly weakened the militant force. Why fight to obtain at best a meagre salary increase if one could achieve more by working for a few months in the Gulf states, in Libya or in Iraq? As usual, emigration encouraged the search for individual solutions and weakened the collective fight. Now that emigration is stemmed, are there any signs of a possible recourse to the Egyptian tradition of collective solutions? The new laws deregulating the labour market in turn weakened the unions, thereby paving the way for wholesale unemployment. This policy, which generated poverty, has so far not appealed to the champions of democracy among the authorities of the globalized system! Many indices indicate a resumption of the struggles. The actions, often violent, are henceforth to be counted in thousands and no longer in hundreds but these will always be scattered. In 1998, seventy strike actions took place in the largest enterprises of the country. The forceful intervention by the special security forces in each of these strikes was difficult to conceal. Some modest victories were recorded here and there. Very little is said about such events. The political parties are silent about their subject. Nobody – of course not even the Islamists – wants to take the risk of being credited with such struggles. The working-class struggles remain isolated but are neither unknown nor unpopular.

In the rural areas, Nasserism operated through some fifteen thousand cooperatives. Although dependent on factions of the middle peasantry and mostly influenced by its rich components, these cooperatives were not chambers for recording decisions taken by the Minister of Agriculture, as often claimed, but rather partners whose views were taken into account. This made it possible to avoid conflicts and marginalize the poor classes among the peasantry. The new liberal policy – suppression of subsidies, credit liberalization and the increase of interest rates from 5 per cent to 14 per cent, a threefold increase in the rates of ground rent and finally the liberalization of relations between landowners and tenants (the rights of tenants were guaranteed until then by the renewal of leases) – broke up the cooperative movement, enabled the rich peasantry to get richer while the middle classes became more impoverished. The frequent but isolated acts of violence that accompanied this change of direction did not prevent the implementation of the liberalization process. In 1993, Tagammu did attempt to establish a new 'Peasants' Union'. However, it withdrew after harassment by the administrative authorities. This did not prevent the protest movement of the majority of tenants from assuming an unexpected dimension in 1998. Nevertheless, the government made manoeuvres, granted concessions to some parties at the expense of others and neutralized the movement (provisionally?) with these tactics. In taking a stand openly in favour of owners in the name of the sacrosanct right to property, the Muslim Brotherhood deliberately aligned themselves with the rural rich, just as they did with the urban compradors, since they were primarily concerned about preserving their image as the valid intermediary for dominant capital and American diplomacy. Their discourse appealed only to the middle classes (as will be seen through the efforts they made in the professional associations), by assigning 'radical' Islamic organizations (Islamic Jihad and others), to recruit their henchmen among the poor middle classes and the lumpen proletariat. In avoiding attempts to defend or condemn these organizations, the Muslim Brotherhood knew that the state destabilization operations conducted by these organizations objectively strengthened them, in their capacity as candidates for the 'changeover'. The Muslim Brotherhood continues to convince their interlocutors that they alone – in power – would be able to put an end to the 'terrorist' transgressions.

The discourse and action of political Islam therefore target the middle classes as a matter of priority. The latter's expansion enhanced the organizations' exceptional influence in the political life of the country. There are twenty-three big professional associations (lawyers, doctors, journalists, engineers, pharmacists, teachers, etc.) with hundreds of thousands of members and a large number of networks of local agencies. Nasserism controlled, without much difficulty, these entities that pre-eminently constitute the mass of principal beneficiaries of populist socio-economic growth. The social crisis fomented by the liberal economic option offered political Islam the opportunity to assume leadership of many of these associations, all the more so as these associations have traditionally been among the places for increased verbal polarization on account of the lack of general debate among the parties. In 1993, the state reacted by taking legislative provisions that enabled it to bring the hostile associations again under control. Demagogic to some extent, the official discourse emphasizes the fact that the associations are 'politicized' at the expense of their concentration on defending the real interests of the professions, which is true. It remains to be seen whether the actual defence of these interests did not in turn conflict with the liberal policies of the state! That could be the starting point for a promising militant action in favour of the Egyptian leftists.

The outburst of community life offered the opportunity for the formation of new 'businessmen' associations. The ancient 'Industrial and Commercial Society' dispersed by Nasser, and the Chambers of Commerce having lost their functions during the planning period, the new businessmen associations filled a real gap. There is much talk about them and they are presented as the proof of the vitality of capitalism. The reality is very different, for it concerned only a clique of 'political rent seekers'. However, their impact in real life is far from negligible.

The student movement had traditionally played a leading role in Egypt, in the Arab world as well as in the Third World as a whole. It was the forum for a dominant communist influence for decades. Even during the glorious period of Nasserism, when this system was accorded prestige and respect, the Nasserian students themselves were identified with the left wing of the regime. They belonged to those mobilized after the 1967 defeat to advocate radicalization of the regime while Nasser himself chose, on the contrary, to make concessions to the right by initiating the *'infitah'*. There is no longer any student movement. This evolution witnessed nearly all over the contemporary Third World has complex sources. The tremendous expansion of the middle classes, which is the outcome of the wave of post-war national liberation struggles, as well as the number of universities, actually has its share of responsibility in this depoliticization process. However, this process was often aided by the authorities' option for systematic repression. That is the case of Egypt. Before and after Nasser, the government deliberately supported the establishment of the Muslim Brotherhood in the university so as to prevent communism, through substantial external funding (by sources in the Gulf states). Moreover, Nasser's 'modernization' of the Azhar University considerably broadened the spectrum opened to the teachings of obscurantists who have their share of responsibility for the drift. The fact remains that the university still plunges into a state of unrest from time to time, but exclusively in matters concerning the Palestinian question, and there is no longer any mobilization for criticisms against the liberal economic and social policies. The aggravation of the social crisis, the worsening situation of middle classes and decline of outlets for graduates have reinforced the instinct for survival, all the more so as the deteriorating quality of education henceforth compromises the analytic potential previously possessed by the youth. The penetration of Islam is the outcome rather than the cause of this drift.

The worlds of the press, intellectuals and artists (especially filmmakers), writers (poets and novelists) have always been present and active on the Egyptian political scene. In the Nasserian era, *Al Ahram*, the institution then headed by Hassanein Heykal, was considered as one of the 'power centres' that enjoyed a certain dose of tolerance *vis-à-vis* the enlightened despot. Due to the high quality maintained by *Al Ahram* (a 125-year-old daily comparable to the world's leading newspapers in terms of quality), and its think tanks, these media currently have insignificant influence in the Egyptian society. The mass media – especially the television organizations – are henceforth vying for monopoly of the empty official discourse and an Islamist propaganda equally mediocre and obscurantist. Yet the few 'independent' television channels operate a self-censorship that annihilates its potential scope – those of all the Arab countries are no better, with the exception of Lebanon's copious network of political television channels. Qatar's new television outfit (Al Khaleej) owes its success to its hosting of lively debates, even though this medium's channels are carefully closed to any leftist radical criticism. Egypt still boasts a quality film industry, even if large-scale commercial production often obscures its existence. Literature – Egypt is a country of novelists, most of them of considerable merit – also has substantial cultural and political influence. Cinema and novels constitute the mainstay of the survival of Egypt's analytical political culture.

Lack of democratic management reflected in virtually all forms of political and social organizations – parties, workers' unions, professional organizations and in the new developing community life – is a major negative feature of Egypt, and perhaps of other Arab countries. These institutions have more quasi-irremovable 'historic heads' than militants.

To complete this picture of struggles, it is worth pointing to the increasing emergence of new forms of struggles by the poorest classes that are barely noticeable because isolated from the visible organizations. The world of street vendors, car park attendants and squatters is no longer an 'unorganized informal sector'. Initially combated for infringing formal rules and regulations, the poor social classes finally asserted themselves – through collective action – and made their claims heard to such an extent that the state renounced the initially scheduled destruction of shanty towns in Cairo, which it replaced with development projects (water supply, road works, etc.).

Syria and Iraq In Syria and Iraq, the Baathist Party initiated similar populist experiments. Unlike in Egypt, whose evolution in this perspective had been triggered by the Free Officers' military coup d'état, without any partisan preparation, the Baath remained the central pole for the political organization of Syria and Iraq (whereas the Socialist Union of Egypt never really existed). The military nature of the Syrian and Iraqi regimes led to an infiltration of armies by the Baath (or its segments). In Egypt, Nasser gradually imposed the populist option against the majority of leaders from among the Free Officers – rather reactionary – but these conflicts at the summit were not transferred at any time into the army, which remained disciplined. There is only one pharaoh in Egypt, just as there is only one emperor in China. Thus, the system prevailing in the Baathist model is rather of the nature of a Baathist-military-mercantile auto-cratic complex in which the rhetoric of Baathism (Arabism initially) fulfilled functions similar to that of the religious discourse elsewhere. The conflict between this model of autocratic power and political Islam therefore assumed more violent dimensions whereas in Egypt the interpenetration of the two forces at play in the post-Nasserian system operated differently.

Since the Baathist model initially had at least a real partisan base, it consequently became 'more efficient' in its dictatorial practices: bringing to heel the dissident political organizations (just as was done to at least some of the Syrian and Iraqi communists), destroying opponents (bourgeois liberals, non-compliant communists, Muslim Brotherhood), absolutely subjugating the social organizations (by suppressing all activities at grassroots level, in the workers' unions for instance), whereas in Egypt the regime had to make do with them. The system's weaknesses are attributed to other equally objective factors, particularly specific regional characteristics and the ethnic and religious diversity of the two countries. This diversity was man-aged in a dubious manner, to say the least, if not unskilfully, in any case, without giving a single thought to the principles of democracy. The supreme leaders' personal qualities and flaws were therefore instrumental and became a determining factor. A typical example was Hafez El Assad, a patient, diplomatic and intelligent leader in Syria, who incidentally had direct confrontation with Israeli expansionism, of which he managed to contain the strategic ambitions through firm resistance without falling into the illusions of 'negotiated solu-tions' under the guidance of American diplomacy. As regards Iraq, a series of murderous military officers – from Abdel Salam Aref to Saddam Hussein – led their country to the tragic impasse in which it finds itself today.

The initial populism has faded away. The military-mercantile complex has embarked on an '*infitah*', unconfirmed but visible in the eyes of the public opinion. The legitimacy and credibility of the original vision of society and of the attendant Pan-Arab discourse are therefore considerably eroded. The political and social struggles are resurfacing actively. The fact that a thousand Syrian intellectuals signed a petition pressing for democracy, without facing repression (a novelty), probably foreshadows the starting point.

Algeria Algeria had a different history. Here, the national liberation struggle assumed another dimension under the leadership of the National Liberation Front (FLN), an authentic and powerful party comparable, at this level, to the communist parties of China or Vietnam even if it was distinguished by its ideology (actually limited to the national claim), its vision of society (or rather the absence of the latter) and therefore by the social content of the resultant power. Similarly, it can be said that national awareness in Algeria has been the result of this struggle and that the Algerian nation and FLN have therefore become synonymous.

The tragedy stemmed from the rapid substitution of the FLN with the ALN (the army, a border unit that had not been the mainspring of the FLN struggle) from July 1962, or probably earlier, and subsequently at the time of Boumédienne. Hoisted at the summits of power, the exclusive centre for final decisions, the army destroyed the legitimacy and credibility of the FLN. The Algerian populism did not outlive Boumédienne. In choosing Chadli to succeed Boumédienne, the army ceased to be unified and disciplined, as each of its generals grabbed a segment of the military-mercantile powers – the mameluke way. Algeria entered into a period of turbulence, serious political conflicts and repeated social struggles that simultaneously produced the worst (the reality to date) but also the best possible results (without that being the outcome of a fake and groundless optimism). The Algerian people aspire to political and social democracy probably more than any other Arab people. This aspiration certainly dates back to the colonial era, to the ambiguity of its discourse and to the forms of resistance it generated. Not even the FLN populism of the glorious era of Boumédienne's short reign could really curtail such an aspiration. The Algerian Charter of 1964 (true copy of the Nasserian model promulgated in 1961), revised in 1976, asserted a few major principles aimed at merging social interests, which were not being granted recognition because of their alleged conflicting nature. In reality therefore, other 'power centres' had to be recognized (in the Egyptian fashion). The first comprised workers' unions, which were important, active and demanding (at least at the grassroots level) with rebellious militants in the bureaucratically imposed departments. Improperly subjected to the FLN, they became active during the last few years; now, thousands of strike actions and 'incidents' are recorded each year. On the other hand, the peasantry, brutalized and altogether destroyed by colonization and the liberation war, could not assert itself as an autonomous force, in spite of the hopes initially placed in the 'self-management' of domains recovered from colonization in the 1960s. That is why the 'agrarian revolution' proclaimed by Boumédienne was a binding official order that did not depend on the support of any peasant movement. It was later smashed silently, in the same way as it was 'made'. Otherwise, the peasant question found expression in the ethnic diversity – through perpetuation of the Berber phenomenon. But here too, the deplorable management of this real diversity as part of a poorly designed Arabization policy, and the constant negation of the problem in the tradition of autocratic powers, produced no results other than making the problem explode through many crises.

Another explosion that foreshadowed crisis took place in 1988 in the form of an action taken by the low-class urban population and particularly its marginalized youths without any future, whose more than deplorable conditions worsened as the new liberal policies abolished the vestiges of the social populism. It was therefore not a revolt of the 'working class', neither a 'peasant rebellion' nor a movement of middle classes and intellectuals demanding political democracy, but actually an explosion of new categories of victims of contemporary capitalism, people without any tradition of organization and without any ideological culture. It is therefore understandable if this outburst, which imposed the recourse to elections (1992), obviously ended in deadlock. For one thing, patrons of the 'Islamist movement' were intelligent enough to understand that they had all their chances in the process. A furious electorate chose to say 'no' to the ruling authority, by saying 'yes' to the Islamists, who therefore presented themselves as the sole visible alternative. The ruling authority opted to fight back but proved incapable of reforming or had no intention of doing so. Therefore Algeria landed in the infernal cycle created by two opposing accomplices who wanted to ensure that the sole option left for the people would be 'them' or 'us'. There is no need to say more about the assassinations for which the Islamists claimed responsibility, particularly those perpetrated against journalists, teachers and democratic artists – personalities who could constitute the third and sole valid choice. There is no need to recall that the massacre of villagers in Mitidja enabled agribusiness speculators to 'buy up' the best lands of the country at zero prices. Unlike the writings of several foreign analysts, it is Yasmina Khadra's novels that give a better insight into the nature of the logic dictating the option for political Islam.

However, the 1988 explosion created such a shock that from 1989, the law authorized reforms in the country's political life. Fifty political parties, 55,000 associations were registered. What is looming on the horizon, beyond the figures that astonish observers, lies in both the range of aspirations to political and social democracy and the objective possibility of their crystallizing around a 'third force' that is potentially the most powerful. That phenomenon has not materialized to date for reasons that are difficult to accept – personal conflict between resurrected 'historic leaders'. The proliferation of associations actually engaged in the fight for democracy and social reforms – in defence of human rights, against torture and deliberate killings, for revision of the family law, for cultural rights of the Berber people, etc. – do not constitute an alternative to the fundamental shortage of leaders. Not more than the increasing working-class struggles pointed out earlier on.

Unfortunately, what is lacking is a unified tribune from which an alternative could be developed in all of its dimensions: defining an authentic economic and social development policy (that will not be pure rhetoric or the expression of a populist nostalgia), defining a new citizenship, a specific code of democratic rights, defining a modern nationality, at the same time Arab and respectful of the Berber reality, defining terms of compromises between the conflicting interests of the social classes and groups, defining the role of the state and linkages with the global system. This is a lot to ask.

Sudan Sudan presents two major contradictions, which have not found a solution – and will not find any – through the acts of violence perpetrated for half a century. Political Islam – in power here – has proved in turn that it is incapable of finding a solution.

The first of these contradictions opposes the rural world of the Arab-Islamic north to its urban counterpart. Sudan's rural areas are closely managed by two brotherhoods – the Ansar and the Khatmia – based on a dominant model in the African Sahel from Senegal to the Red Sea. The two major political parties (Mahdists and National Democratic Party), which are closely linked to frontiers of the brotherhoods (and constitute the historical Islam actually existing in Sudan), are therefore assured of their victory in any election, even though they obviously have no programme apart from the one aimed at managing society as it is. On the contrary, the urban sector is surprisingly developed: there are powerful workers' unions (particularly that of the railways sector, vital to this vast country), a vanguard students' union, professional organizations comprising active and democratic middle classes (an exception or almost unique in the Arab world), blossoming community life involving women's movements, the strong ideological influence of the communist party. This contradiction is insoluble, for it commands the changeover from military dictatorships, behind which are rallied the two brotherhoods, amid popular democratic demonstrations provisionally terminating the existing system.

The second contradiction in Sudan opposes 30 million inhabitants of the Arab-Muslim north to the religiously different south (with between a quarter and one-third of the population). Sudanese governments are unable to consider managing this contradiction otherwise than through constant war, whereas it is not difficult to think up a solution based on democracy, local autonomy and recognition of diversity. At any rate, this solution is advocated by all the democratic forces of the north, particularly the communist party, and was even implemented by these forces for very short periods (never exceeding a few months) in places where they wield power, only to be called into question by reactionary forces ever ready to use violence in toppling the former group. This solution is also recommended by political forces of the south, whose army – under John Garang – is designated as the Sudan People's Liberation Army (without reference to secession), not by chance.

The intrusion of political Islam has been the outcome of weariness due to repeated failures, massive injection of Saudi financial resources (channelled through a powerful mercantile class itself affiliated to the brotherhoods), and the tactical genius of a very ambitious power-hungry religious fanatic (Hassan Turabi). In concluding an alliance directly with the military dictatorship (of Numeiri, and subsequently of Beshir) while short-circuiting the brotherhoods, Turabi dreamt (or, while seeking in reality to entrench his power, pretended to be dreaming) about 'purging' and 'wahabizing' the country's political Islam (hence, the support enlisted from Saudi Arabia). The resources used by the military-Islamic dictatorship were therefore meant to be 'modern' and to put an end to the 'toleration' of the historic brotherhood Islam. This explains the series of harsh laws prohibiting free union activity (1992), subjugating community life (especially the blossoming of associations in charge of humanitarian relief operations in this country plagued with war and famine – the law of 1995), gagging the press (law of 1996), etc. The fact remains that all the attempts made to substitute a network of new 'modern' institutions – controlled by Turabi's personal power – for the prohibited democratic organizations produced no result, strictly speaking. The few 'NGOs' that appeared to survive the massacre have been retrieved and assimilated by the brotherhoods.

Obviously, the regime's economic and social action could end only in disaster: totally subjected to the logic of globalized liberalism, to the extent of caricaturing the political racketeering of the military-Islamic-mercantile clans, the political Islam in power in Sudan only contributed to a gruesome aggravation of all the problems. The regime adopted just a 'casual attitude' towards this drift by allowing the south war to peter out, by allowing all the western provinces (Kordofan, Darfur) – mainly Muslim – and the eastern provinces (Kassala) to be governed by way of semi-secession. The regime's main concern has been to keep up appearances by remaining masters of the street in the capital and in the immediate neighbourhoods. Its principal achievement therefore consisted in creating the so-called 'people's defence' and 'student security' networks recruited among the lumpen, to terrorize people, and nothing more, in the Iranian Pasdaran fashion. The Achilles' heel of the system is its total lack of any form of legitimacy allowing for political succession. An Islamic power other than the brotherhoods will have much difficulty taking roots in Sudan, unlike in Iran, where the 'wilaya al faqih' is supported by a real national church (Shiite in this case) established as an institution dominating the state, in contrast to Saudi Arabia, whose monarchy links up tribal legitimacy and that of the Wahabite version of Islam, or Morocco, whose monarchy is both national and religious in character. The democratic opposition is not dead. It has survived all the brutalities of political Islam. However, virtually all of its directorates have been compelled to go into exile in Egypt, which hosts the National Democratic Alliance of Sudan, created in Asmara in 1995 from the merger of all the parties and organizations prohibited in Sudan. Egypt, which has never thought of treating Sudanese nationals as aliens, has therefore received an indefinite number of emigrants estimated at 2 million at least (the majority being ordinary workers obviously fleeing their country's declining economic life). At any rate, the potentially powerful front has no programme enabling it to coordinate struggles – which remain isolated but frequent in the country – and strengthen their capacity to crystallize into an alternative.

Morocco Based on a twofold national and religious legitimacy, the Moroccan monarchy encouraged guaranteed democratic break-throughs so long as they pleased the king. Moreover, such initiatives have the advantage of not threatening the local dominant classes or the global system. However, it must not be forgotten that the growing contradiction between hopes nurtured by these positive developments on the one hand and the symptoms of social crisis, which the system of options associated with the democracy in question does not even make it possible to attenuate, on the other hand, may cause a violent explosion one day.

Whereas elsewhere – in Egypt, Tunisia and Iraq for example – national liberation struggles were compelled to distance themselves from or even to oppose the local monarchies, in Morocco, things were different. Istiqlal – the movement's conservative wing – which dominated the political scene for a long time and never became negligible even subsequently, intended to do nothing more than restoring Morocco's sovereignty and monarchy. The modernist wing itself was compelled to hush up its possible points of view on the question of monarchy. This modernist wing had many bases in the country. These included powerful workers' unions that remained so, despite the erosive effects of economic liberalization and unemployment, and even managed to safeguard their autonomy not only *vis-à-vis* the state (which never sought to subjugate them – since it was not a populist state) but also *vis-à-vis* its political allies and defenders (UNFP, which became USFP, and the communist party, now PPS), the growing middle class itself, which aspires to attain portions of the power monopolized by the Maghzen (the court) and the peripheral business bourgeoisie groups, themselves excluded from the Maghzen.

The phases of graduated concessions made by the monarchy to these forces are well known: from the first parliamentary elections of

1963 to the constitutional amendments of 1962 and 1996, from the first 'democratic' experiences (that is, in accepting that the government emerged from relatively fair elections) to the one that brought USFP and its leader, Abdel Rahman Youssofi, into the government in 1998, it is said that the system is developing into a parliamentary monarchy, which will preserve its religious aura. But, after all, the Queen of England is actually the head of the Anglican Church, is she not? The Moroccan establishment therefore has no serious political problems. The Moroccan middle classes have no 'problem of identity', unlike in neighbouring Algeria. The Moroccan system has managed cultural-ethnic diversity without provoking cleavages in the nation, according to the traditional principle of duality between the Maghzen (urban areas and neighbouring countryside)/Bled Siba (distant countryside, the majority being of the Berber stock), while the king renews tribal allegiance without ever touching the autonomy of the local chieftainships. In taking the initiative to promote Amazigi culture and language, the Moroccan system never considered that there could be a contradiction between Arabity, Islam and the Berber reality. Political Islam, which is trying to make a breakthrough here, just as it has elsewhere, is confronted with a Maghzen religious legitimacy, which it has been unable to call into question to date. On the other hand, however, the ruling power is confronted with social problems that are assuming increasingly serious dimensions, as none of the country's successive governments, not even those that can rightly boast about democratic legitimacy, ever tried to get out of the rut of globalized liberalism. It is therefore no accident if here, too, the repeated explosions are the work of the urban poor, the new class of victims of modern capitalism. These explosions are contained or repressed with violence amid the silence of the leading democratic forces. But for how long?

The 'third sector' of the social reality

This section focuses again on one of the terms circulated by the dominant modes of the contemporary discourse. Like all these expressions – for which synonyms are substituted interchangeably, such as 'civil society', among others – this term is vague and ambiguous, as it refers to aspects of reality that are by no means new, but also to new ones, without any attempt to distinguish between them.

Everybody knows more or less the meaning of state or state

power from which all the institutions can be identified. Everyone also knows what the 'world of business' implies in our capitalist system; in other words, all the production units for marketable goods and services dictated by the logic of cost-effectiveness and profit based on the principle of capitalist economy (private ownership and the right to compete in markets). But it is obvious that social reality cannot be limited to the two poles formed by the state and the private sector (if that is the name for units forming the capitalist economy). The socio-political life of individuals and groups is also expressed through other means and other formal or informal forms of organization.

Such a platitude – valid at all times and in all places – may not deserve to be proposed as a 'discovery' of a reality that might be 'new' and worthy of the name, be it the 'third sector' or 'civil society'. But behind this linguistic innovation of the dominant discourse is an ideology that must be deconstructed.

In the pre-modern societies of Europe, as in the Islamic world, churches or the Islamic institution assumed major responsibilities, for example in the education and health sectors. To this effect, religious institutions had their own funds (almost fiscal returns). The same applied to the corporate bodies, through which technological knowledge was transmitted. The secularization of the modern European state and expansion of marketable services did not necessarily blot out this role of the churches. In countries where the Protestant Reformation triumphed, churches were really 'nationalized' – and almost placed under state control – thereby preserving at least part of these functions now financed through government subsidies taken from their own previous resources including those realized from the exploitation of agricultural estates expropriated from the church. Even in France, where the secular revolution was more radical, the church enjoyed a quasi-monopoly of primary education until the early twentieth century and still administers the management of part of the education sector now subsidized by the state. Set between public service and the commercial exercise of a free medical profession, the health sector became a public utility only with the generalization of the welfare state after the Second World War. At the same time, the purely mercantile character of the supply of such services remained quite marginal until the neoliberal offensive of the last twenty years. The case was different in the United States, where the 'local communities' (which were themselves often confused with various religious communities) and the commercial private sector have always provided most of the services considered.

The Arab and Islamic world had a similar history and the vestiges of these ancient systems have been kept very much alive to date. For want of specific organization like that of the Catholic or Orthodox churches, the religious institution was subjected as much as possible to state power wielded by the caliph or local sultans. In areas where this institution assumed a format close to that of the church – in Shiite Iran – the latter was placed under the supervision of the Shah's state (from the time of the Sefevids in the eighteenth century). Iran's Islamic revolution merely reversed the relationships by subjecting the state to the religious institution.

In the Sunni world, lack of autonomous organization of the given religious institution facilitated the proliferation of 'brotherhoods' – Sufis or others – who always sought to be independent of the state power that fought or suppressed them as systematically as possible. Even in the so-called secular Kemal's Turkey, the Islamic institution was actually controlled by the state and was never suppressed or even 'ignored', as is often claimed. In this context, Kemalism pursued the same objectives as did the Ottoman sultanate – by intrumentalizing religion and subjecting it to the sultanate's objectives.

Nothing of that sort disappeared in the contemporary Arab and Islamic world, either as a result of colonization in North Africa, the 'bourgeois' regimes marking the period between the two wars in Egypt and the Mashreq or those of the populist nationalism that spanned the second half of the twentieth century. In Morocco, there are still more than five thousand *habous* (the equivalent of Mashreq *waqfs*) – significant properties in mortmain – whose revenues are the dominant source whereby non-state and unofficial market services were financed. Renamed as 'non-governmental organizations' (NGOs), the said 'associations' are mere inheritors of the ancient *habous*. In Sudan, the two principal brotherhoods (Ansar and Khatmia), which turned into 'political parties', are also looming behind the majority of 'NGOs' that provide social services. The frenzied attempts by an 'Islamic' authority, which claimed to be 'fundamentalist' and therefore ignored the brotherhoods, have so far yielded meagre results. In the Mashreq countries (Egypt, Syria and Iraq), the regimes of populist nationalism actually suppressed the *waqfs* (as had been the case in Kemal's Turkey) but they then brought the Islamic institution under state control. The regimes of this same populist nationalism had of course given the state monopoly in the provision of social services but the state itself always integrated the religious institution, which then appeared to be completely subjugated.

Moreover, the contemporary era is marked by a capital-based offensive intended to open new horizons for its expansion, precisely those managed to date in the unofficial market framework, either by the public utility or by religious and community institutions, which do not adequately meet the criteria for 'association'. In what way are linkages established between the possible expansion of the community organization ('NGO') – which is itself incorporated into or outside the religious institution – and the expansion of the values and criteria of the free-enterprise economy? How are the concepts of public service and those defining the market rationality henceforth interrelated or conflicting? These are some of the questions veiled by the 'anti-state' rhetoric, which we have to discuss openly.

The propagandists of liberal theory pronounce on this subject – their strong point – but nevertheless without any scientific foundation or empirical basis. According to this discourse, the communities (that define community life) and the commercial private sector might be more capable of providing the social services required by society than the public service. State might actually be synonymous with absurd bureaucracy in the best of cases, and often with tyranny, the source of irresponsible wastage, as the costs of the services it administers are diluted in the national budget. On the contrary, the communities or *a fortiori* the commercial private sector should and can actually count, when it comes to matters concerning their money. They know perfectly how to adapt to the various needs, as they are flexible by nature. Unlike the state, community organizations and the private sector would therefore be higher expressions of the exercise of democracy, transparency and accountability. The democracy in question refers to freedom in the sense that Von Hayek gives to this unique value: it is that of the freedom of the strongest parties; it ignores the other value – that of equality – without which there is no democracy. Von Hayek is a rightist libertarian and not a democrat.

On the contrary, the reality shows the indisputable superiority of the public service in relation to community organizations and the private sector (the comparison being meaningful only if its terms are situated within the same society or societies with comparable levels of general development and wealth). Expenditure on the highly privatized health sector in the United States absorbs 14 per cent of the country's GDP as against 7 per cent in Europe, whose results measured in terms of infant mortality and life expectancy are much higher, especially because, in Europe, health comes mainly under public service, to say nothing about the disparities, which are more flagrant in the United States, whose citizens have the right to health care commensurate with their wallet. On the other hand, the privatization of health care guarantees substantial profits for the pharmaceutical and medical industries, as it does for American insurance companies, which do not compare with their European counterparts. It is therefore a question of wastage of which the scope exceeds, by far, what can be attributed to the bureaucracies and excesses of public social security recipients. As for transparency and financial accountability, they are less difficult to enforce in the public service than in the private sector, which enjoys professional secrecy, and this can in principle be raised and examined in Parliament in an effective democratic system.

The liberal theory in this field is therefore neither a theory nor the outcome of empirical observation. It is pure propaganda, in the basest sense of the term; in other words, it is a lie. In fact, behind this propaganda looms the conflict between two concepts of the management of social services. On the one hand lies the originally British concept – which ignores that of public service – exported and carried to extremes in the United States of America. On the other hand is the public service, which is predominant in modern culture, not only in France, but also in many of the countries of the European mainland. The Anglo-American concept subjects all aspects of social life to the priority and exclusive requirements for the expansion of the field managed by dominant capital. The Franco-European concept limits the inherent devastating effects. The Arab debates on these issues are at the heart of the discussions and conflicting policy-related propositions witnessed in the Arab world.

Community associations: a genuine burgeoning or a smokescreen?

The burgeoning of community associations over the last twenty years in the Arab world, as everywhere else, cannot be denied. The statistics – approximate and always greatly underestimated – give figures of 55,000 NGOs registered in Algeria, 15,000 in Egypt, 18,000 in Morocco and, for the Arab world as a whole, probably over 100,000. These figures have been multiplied by a coefficient varying from five to ten, according to country, for the last twenty years.

A majority of the NGOs (almost all those surveyed) receive 'private' subsidies of local origin (i.e. not from abroad). These subsidies are considerable for the largest organizations working in the field of education, health and other social services, or qualified as such. They come from *habous* (in Morocco), or the network of Islamic economic institutions (including Islamic banks), or 'benefactors' who are in fact millionaires belonging to the Islamic tendency of the state/business network. Funds from the oil-rich Gulf form part of this support, of which the Islamic-linked organizations are the only beneficiaries.

Another source of finance comes from the sale of services of which one-third of the NGOs are beneficiaries, but particularly the most important of them, working in education and health. Many NGOs do indeed undertake activities that are purely commercial, even if they present themselves as 'benefactors of humanity'. Here again, confusion between the various political and ideological activities of an Islamic nature is common.

Then, finally, there is external assistance, both from foreign governments (or foreign institutions), and from institutions related to international organizations (particularly the World Bank, UNDP and European development assistance). These are not much better documented than other sources of funding. A third of the NGOs benefit from them. Control by the state authorities is nitpicking in Arab countries and almost everywhere authorization is required before foreign subsidies can be accepted. The security services could thus make this valuable information available, but they do not do so. However, it seems likely that, as far as Egypt is concerned at least, the main donor is USAID, which has a 'special' agreement with Egypt, and its support goes to a large group of NGOs of medium size, involved in supplying services and development projects which are looked on favourably both by the authorities (they also benefit from public subsidies) and by the Islamic tendency (to which many of them claim allegiance). It also seems that donors from European communities (particularly the Netherlands) are active in northern Africa, Lebanon and Palestine.

Transparency and accountability certainly do not characterize the way NGOs are funded. In contrast to common perceptions of them, they form a collection of institutions and activities that are far more impenetrable than the organizations and activities of the public sector, the budgets of which are at least published and available.

The NGOs operate under the close scrutiny of the state, although this is not altogether true in the case of Lebanon and Palestine. The democratic principle, according to which the creation of associations is free, means that the state does not have the right to intervene (which could result in prohibition) except for reasons that have to be spelt out legally and fall under the control of tribunals: this does not apply in the Arab world. On the contrary, the principle of authorization in advance is the general rule.

The NGO networks are active in different fields, but it is relatively easy to group them into five main categories.

The first carries out a series of interventions in fields that are normally within the jurisdiction of the state (education, health, social services). They take up a major part of the funds received by associations (more than two-thirds of the total). The surveys carried out in the Arab countries as a whole make it possible to give an idea of the relative importance of the different social services supplied by this 'third sector' of social life. Education and training, from school to university, and various professional specializations head the list. Not far behind are all the services connected with health, children, family planning and other such social services.

Public subsidies and those of foreign donors are more frequent in this context than in the fields of education and health, as such. The reason is that these programmes are generally conceived – if only to attract support – in the terms laid down by the fashions concerning the 'war on poverty'. The support of the Islamic movements – and often their control – is both overt and proclaimed.

The second category concerns the activities of NGOs associated with specific development projects; it involves about 15 per cent of the active associations that have been registered. Half of them are for projects in urban areas (small-scale artisan businesses and co-operatives, professional training) and the other half for rural projects. Here, also, the public and external support seems to be decisive, while that of the Islamic movements is apparently marginal.

A third category concerns the organizations engaged in defending people's rights, both the rights of human beings in general, or more particularly workers' rights, or the rights and demands of women.

The fourth category is more particularly concerned with defending the rights – cultural or political – of minorities, as they are referred to in the international 'community', although these associations and their institutions refuse to use the word, since they consider – rightly – that they are segments of national society as a whole. This is the case with the numerous local associations in Morocco, which have been set up to promote *amazigi* culture. The churches – Coptic and others – are acting in the same way, creating many associations to reinforce their ties with their communities.

The fifth category is made up of 'businessmen's associations'; this is a real novelty successfully taken up in a number of Arab countries. They are powerful organizations.

The general arguments for and against community associations are well known and debated in Arab countries as elsewhere. Many of them are formulated in terms too general to be useful in the debate as to whether these activities can open up new prospects – within the limits permitted in the situation of contemporary Arab societies: the political forces they use, the margins of liberty allowed by the autocratic state, the means they employ to go beyond these limits. It is necessary also to take into account the extreme heterogeneity of the associations.

Some observations are in order here, resulting from all the studies and discussions on the subject.

First, ecology has not become a burning issue in the Arab world. We have not come across even one ecological movement worthy of the name in any Arab country. There are only a few ecological organizations and they are merely cliques, without any real activities, motivated by external support and exploited by a few individuals.

Second, feminism has not become a force strong enough to take on the tragic challenge posed by Arab societies. It is important not to confuse women's movements in the real sense of the term (that is, movements that aim at transforming the situation) with the 'participation of women in development'. The defenders of the present system stress statistics that actually mean nothing. In fact, activities supporting education and health benefit women as much as men. The intervention of the Islamic tendencies in these fields only aggravates the situation. Studies carried out on this subject, in Egypt (Azza

Khalil), show that they follow a strategy that aims at reinforcing the submission of women to the law as it exists, in exchange for a small improvement in material conditions, given in a spirit of charity rather than one of according rights.

Third, it is often said that the activities of associations target a public that used to be ignored by the existing dominant modes of life and social action: state, political parties, trade unions. There is little doubt that Arab societies today are very different from what they used to be fifty years ago. The social crisis – the internal polarization that parallels the split at global level created by the expansion of capitalism and exacerbated by the present liberalism – results in between one-third and one-half of the urban population being integrated, but only into what is called the 'informal' economy. And this is accompanied by a rise in poverty, even if it is 'modernized', which affects more than a third of the Arab urban population, if the criteria of the World Bank are used. This modern urban poverty is in addition to the so-called 'traditional' rural poverty (in fact it is not traditional, as it too is the product of capitalist modernization, resulting particularly from its liberal options), which affects an even greater proportion of the population in the countryside.

The question is, therefore, should we insist on the need for another economic, social and political strategy that aims at reabsorbing the marginalized, or can we accept the present situation and try only to adjust and manage it? The dominating discourse would have us believe that the second option is the only 'realistic' one. At the same time it claims to draw a practical conclusion from its observation of the facts. The 'traditional' forms of social struggle, which developed within identifiable workplaces and were often concentrated (factories, administrative services, professions, cooperatives), do not affect more than half the active population, at best. Thus, it is said, they have lost their effectiveness and their credibility. This is true, but only partially so. On the other hand, it is also said, the new social structures put the place where people live – the neighbourhood – at the heart of mobilizing activities. This is not altogether incorrect.

Nevertheless, what really happens in the dominating 'informal' milieu can be criticized. It is true that many of the associations' activities are targeted to this milieu, but surveys show that active participation in projects by beneficiaries has not really been studied. In half of the cases studied in Egypt and other countries, those responsible said that they did not even try to investigate this; the other half found that 'consultation' with those concerned was difficult (and in hardly any cases was there any effective participation). The reasons given for this behaviour are banal: the beneficiaries are ignorant, they do not know what is good for them, etc. This is, no doubt, why the 'spontaneous movements' that develop in these milieux happen outside the associations and are considered (rightly) as 'illegal' actions.

The discourse on 'grassroots action' remains a discourse. It is not surprising, therefore, that those concerned behave like 'clients', a fact that only reinforces the nepotistic attitudes of those in charge. Such attitudes promote the 'depoliticization' of the people involved, their hostility to politics (such as practised in the relationships between associations, or between the state and the associations). They can only reproduce the authoritarian populist traditions that political Islam has taken over.

Fourth, most of the actions that have been studied (the five kinds of intervention considered) are not independent of the state. This 'community life' is therefore largely window-dressing. The only exceptions to the rule are those organizations struggling to promote human rights, social rights and the rights of women.

Studies show that most associations constituting civil society do not complain about the state. As many as 70 per cent of them are satisfied with its 'liberalism', i.e. its support. They are not interested in passing judgment on – or even knowing – the macro-policies within which their actions take place. They are not critical, either, of economic liberalism or of the globalization that serves as its frame of reference. The existing relationships of cooperation between numerous associations and the state not only involve support from public finances, but also the planning of actions, developed in common with administrations considered competent in the field. This loss of autonomy is not seen as being bothersome: it is perhaps caused by the lack of ideas among the leaders of the associations concerned, or perhaps autonomy as an idea has been lacking from the start.

Fifth, the accusation made by the authorities that NGOs constitute a Trojan horse on behalf of imperialism is odd to say the least. Because the Trojan horse is actually the authoritarian mameluke state itself. The discourse of political Islam which addresses the same reproach to the bodies of civil society – of being agents of 'the West'

– is equally strange because, in practice, the Islamists accept globalized liberalism. Those who refuse to accept such strategies – the organizations of resistance and struggle in civil society – are criticized by the state, by political Islam and by foreign institutions!

What conclusions may we draw?

Arab civil society is, as elsewhere, a reflection of the state and political society in the region. It is extremely naïve to oppose the state and political parties – which are decreed 'bad' – and so-called civil society, assumed to possess all the qualities attributed to it by the dominant discourse.

All in all, the actions of civil society have not proved either more effective or better run than those of public service. Looking at them case by case, we find that most of the 'projects' thought up here and there by offices influenced by 'donors' (the World Bank in particular) are badly designed and inappropriate for local conditions. Nor do they solve real problems. The failures are countless. Any comparison between these projects and the activities of state services is more favourable to the latter, in spite of all the criticisms of them.

As for the very terms of the discourse that influence most of these actions, the results are mediocre, to say the least. 'Poverty' is growing. The 'target population' benefiting from these policies remains a small proportion of the whole. As for their 'empowerment', it exists only in the minds of those who hold forth about it.

Most of these actions are therefore in no way 'more effective' than those of the state, nor are they less costly. On top of this they are not transparent, nor are they made accountable – rather less so than in the public sector. And finally they are not managed more efficiently and they are not more democratic.

If this is the case, it is because the basic strategies upon which these actions are founded are also those of the state. In short, they are the strategies of capital that dominate at the world level and at local levels. In no way do they solve the problems of the people involved.

The above is applicable only to the actions as a whole of so-called civil society (and the state) which are based on the (false) principle of consensus and which are therefore in keeping with dominant liberalism. In contrast, the political and social struggles that are carried out within or out of the parties, trade unions, professional associations, organizations struggling for democracy, human rights, the rights of workers and of women, open up the prospect of possible alternatives. This creative aspect of political and civil society engaged in the struggle to transform social relationships is the basis upon which another future can be built – one more equitable and more egalitarian and which gives greater freedom to individuals, peoples and nations.

At present, political and social struggles are fragmented. The ideological void produced by the erosion and finally the collapse of populist nationalism and actually existing socialism has deprived these struggles – in their current state of development – of any prospect of credible alternatives. The dominant discourse encourages people to renounce such struggles and be content with 'managing everyday life'. Postmodernism offers a 'scholarly' version of this ideology of capitulation, while 'good governance' is the popular version.

The only alternative must be based on effective struggles. However, theoretical reflection cannot stand in for the lack of debate at the grassroots. Both are indispensable, but they are effective only when they are combined. 'Recomposing the social (class) struggle' – which defines the objective of this dialectic – means a coming together, based on genuine common interests identified by the groups themselves, identifying the objectives, by stages, that facilitate the move forward and improve the material and moral conditions of these groups. The struggles should be pursued with this end in view. Along the way, struggles carried out in this way encourage the democratic behaviour that is necessary and foster the development of new directions that are authentically rooted in people's own experience.

Geo-strategy, Arab unity and Palestinian *intifadas*

By virtue of its extraordinary oil wealth, which is vital to the economy of the dominant Triad (United States, Europe and Japan), the Middle East has always occupied and continues to occupy a special position in world geopolitics and in the hegemonic military geo-strategy of the United States of America. Moreover, its geographic position along the southern edge of the USSR enhanced its importance during the Cold War era. This trend was taken over – after the collapse of the Soviet regime – by the important oil resources of the ex-Soviet Caucasus and Central Asia, a region which is composed mainly of Muslim countries, where there is constant conflict between the diplomacies of Washington and Moscow.

In the American geo-military configuration of the world, the region represented and continues to represent a zone considered as a top priority (like the Caribbean), in other words an area where the United States has assumed the 'right' of military intervention. At any rate, the United States did so during the Gulf War (1990) and took advantage of that intervention to place the countries concerned under its permanent military protection.

The United States of America operates in the Middle East in collaboration with Turkey and Israel – its two unconditional supporters. Europe has kept out of the region, accepting that the United States alone defends the overall interests of the Triad, that is to say, its oil supply. In spite of some signs of irritation, the Europeans continue to back Washington in the region.

The Arab national populism project did not accept this situation, since its ambition was to impose recognition of the independence of the Arab world by the superpowers. This was the meaning of the 'non-alignment' supported by the Soviets. The page of this epoch now having turned, the Arab world currently has no specific vision of its position in the new global system. This is the reason why the 'projects' concerning the organization of the region are designed elsewhere.

Here too, the United States had taken the initiative in putting forward a strange-looking 'Middle East Common Market' project, in which the Gulf countries would have invested capital while the other Arab countries provided cheap labour and Israel assisted with technological monitoring in addition to assuming the functions of the inevitable intermediary. It was then that Europe tried to react by formulating, in turn, the 'Euro-Mediterranean Partnership' project, also integrating Israel into the plan but excluding the Gulf countries and thus recognizing that their 'management' was the exclusive responsibility of Washington.

These geo-political dimensions cannot be ignored in the debate on political and social struggles. Having analysed them in detail elsewhere, we will only recall their general significance here.

Israel's colonial expansionism poses a real challenge; it is not a figment of the Arab world's imagination. Israel is the only country in the world that refuses to recognize any established borders (and hence should not have the right to be a member of the United Nations). Like the nineteenth-century United States of America,

Israel thinks it has the right to conquer new areas for the expansion of its colonization and to treat the people who have been living there for two thousand years – if not more – like 'Redskins' to be hunted or exterminated. Israel is the only country that has openly declared that it does not feel bound by United Nations resolutions.

The 1967 war, planned in agreement with Washington from 1965 onwards, pursued several objectives: to start working for the decline of populist nationalist regimes, to break up their alliance with the Soviet Union, compelling them to reposition themselves, and to follow in the footsteps of America and open up new lands for Zionist colonization. In the territories conquered in 1967, Israel therefore instituted an apartheid system inspired by that of South Africa. Whenever it is accused of racism – which is clear and overt – Zionism responds by systematically blackmailing critics by accusing them of anti-Semitism. Israel also exploits the 'Holocaust industry'. To carry on with its project, Israel requires an Arab world weakened as much as possible at all levels.

It is here that the interests of globally dominant capital tally with those of Zionism. For one thing, the logic of carrying on with the project of actually existing capitalism has always resulted in and still contributes to polarization on a world scale. The 'development' of any Third World region – in this case, the Arab region – conflicts with that of the global expansion of actually existing capitalism. On the other hand, a modernized, rich and powerful Arab world would call into question Western countries' ability to plunder the region's oil resources as a necessity for the continual wastage inevitably associated with capitalist accumulation. Political authorities in the Triad countries do not want a modernized and powerful Arab world because, by nature, these countries are faithful servants of dominant transnational capital.

The alliance between the Western powers and Israel is therefore built on the solid foundation of their common interests. This alliance is neither the product of a feeling of culpability on the part of the Europeans, who were responsible for anti-Semitism and Nazism, nor that of the 'Jewish lobby's' skill in exploiting this sentiment. Had the Western powers felt that Zionist colonial expansionism did not serve their interests, they would quickly have found ways to overcome their 'complex' and 'neutralize' the 'Jewish lobby'. We have no doubts about this, for we are not among those who naïvely think that public opinion imposes its views on authorities in democratic countries. Everybody knows that public opinion 'is fabricated'; hence, Israel would be unable to resist for more than a couple of days if measures (even moderate ones) involving a blockade were taken against it, just as the Western powers did to Yugoslavia, Iraq and Cuba. It would therefore not be difficult to bring Israel to its senses and create conditions for genuine peace, if the Western powers wanted it. They clearly do *not* want it.

Arab public opinion is not well equipped to understand the nature of the links between the Zionist project and that of the general expansion of capitalism. In this case, Arab public opinion is the victim of the limited scope of populist nationalist thought, the foundations of which it has so far been unable to criticize, let alone to transcend.

After the defeat in 1967, Sadat declared that, since the United States had '90 per cent of the cards' in their game (that was his actual expression), it was necessary to break with the USSR and join the Western camp. The result would be that Washington might be induced to exert sufficient pressure on Israel and thus bring the latter to its senses. Even beyond this 'strategic idea' specific to Sadat – which later developments proved to be flimsy – Arab public opinion remained altogether unable to realize the global process of capitalist expansion, let alone to identify its real contradictions and weaknesses. Is it not alleged and repeated that the 'Westerners will finally realize that their actual interest lies in maintaining sound relations with the two hundred million Arabs – their immediate neighbours – and not in sacrificing such relations for the unconditional support of Israel'? It implies thinking that the 'Westerners' concerned (that is to say dominant capital) wished for a modernized and developed Arab world; it also implies not realizing that Westerners, who want to make the Arab world powerless, consider it expedient to support Israel.

The choice made by Arab governments – apart from those of Syria and Lebanon – which made them subscribe to the American plan for the so-called 'lasting peace' through the Madrid and Oslo negotiations (1993), could not produce any results other than those that it generated: encouraging Israel to carry on with its expansionist project. By openly rejecting the terms of the 'Oslo Agreement' today, Ariel Sharon is displaying just what should have been realized much earlier: the fact that the agreement had nothing to do with a 'lasting peace' but was rather a question of opening a new phase of Zionist colonial expansion.

The permanent state of war imposed on the region by Israel and the Western powers supporting its project in turn constitutes a powerful motive for the perpetuation of the autocratic regimes of Arab countries. This blockage of a possible democratic evolution weakens the opportunities for revival in the Arab world, thereby paving the way for the deployment of dominant capital and the hegemonic strategy of the United States. They have come full circle, for the alliance between Israel and America serves the interests of the two partners.

The fight for democracy and social progress in the Arab world is therefore not contingent on so-called peace plans, which are something else. On the contrary, the effective conduct of this battle is contingent on unveiling the real objectives of these projects to discredit them. It is necessary to identify the arguments that lead to such a conclusion.

The arguments concerning geo-strategy, which we have outlined here, have their limits, for they present only those in the forefront: the dominant forces; in other words, transnational capital and the powers placed at its service. Expressions such as 'Western powers, Western interests' refer to 'the interests of dominant capital'.

However, the latter do not constitute the entirety of social reality; the peoples – indeed all the peoples – equally exist. A strategy for effective struggle against the 'geo-political' logic concerned calls for the unearthing of contradictions between interests of the victims and those of the forces dominating the authorities. This strategy is neither 'easier' in the West – because democracy would help towards its rapid deployment – nor 'easier' in the East, because the violence of the destructive effects of capitalist expansion there is more obvious. It is difficult here and there, although they are different for specific reasons. However, there is no possible alternative to taking this initiative. It is because, at the end of the deployment of the globalized liberal capitalist project, there is apartheid on a world scale and, in its framework, the apartheid imposed on Palestinians by Zionism. Creating a global front in support of the Palestinian people fighting against apartheid is not only a moral duty but also an important dimension of a strategy for effective war against capitalist dictatorship;

it also constitutes a real contribution in support of the Arab peoples' struggle for democracy and social progress.

Pan-Arabism is both a reality and a positive phenomenon. Given the cultural destruction and other effects of the globalization process, as it is, if the French-speaking community, the Portuguese-speaking community and the spirit of the Latin American family are frameworks for legitimate resistance (and they are, in my opinion), then what is the basis for sniggering at Pan-Africanism or Pan-Arabism? Why should the familiarity between peoples occupying a territory stretching from the Atlantic to the Gulf and using the same language (despite the variants of the local languages) be devoid of significance and interest?

Yet, saying that there is 'only one Arab nation' divided up against its will entails a discrepancy that should be avoided. It is because this national question remains infinitely more complex than what the ideology of 'Arab nationalism' connotes (*qawmi*, as opposed to *qutri*, concerning the frameworks defined by the borders of the Arab states). The national reality of the Arab peoples is expressed in terms of the overlapping stages of a pyramid. The Pan-Arab dimension (*qawmi*) is a reality. But the 'local' dimensions (*qutri*) are no less a reality. In fact, if it is true that the demarcation of historical Syria (the present-day territories of Syria, Lebanon, Palestine and Jordan) is recent (1919), artificial and is actually the outcome of an imperialist partition, like that of the fertile crescent (historical Syria and Iraq), it would be ridiculous to claim that Egypt, Morocco and Yemen are artificial and recent fabrications. Whether ancient or new, the expression 'local nation' (*qutri*) is based on the interests and real perceptions of their specific characteristics.

The national liberation movements and the populist nationalisms they generated were deployed on the basis of such realities in the states just as they are. The internal development strategies they wanted to establish on self-centred foundations – so as to modernize their societies, transform them progressively and assert their autonomy vis-à-vis imperialism – could be nothing other than what they were: designed and implemented in the states (*qutri*).

The Pan-Arab dimension could have called for implementation of complementary strategies aimed at strengthening each partner's internal structures and not those to be substituted for such structures. This was not the case, because the representatives of populist nationalisms were not equipped efficiently to design such complementarity, their perception of the real nature of the modern capitalist challenge being what it used to be: insufficient, to say the least. This is why all that the 'technocrats' in their service could conceive of was nothing other than 'common markets' which, to be precise, is a capitalist strategy that is absolutely inappropriate.

At the political level, the same limitations of both populism and the autocratic state accounted for the failures. The Baath, which presented itself as the promoter of 'Arabness' (ourouba), was unable to go beyond rhetoric and the analogy with the experiences of Germany and Italy, which were caricatured without the least awareness of the fact that the conditions on the periphery of the system in the twentieth century were not those of nineteenth-century Europe!

The official Pan-Arabism of the populist authorities has been overtaken leftwards for a while by the qawmiyin movement, a group of young revolutionaries imbued with Marxism, Maoism and Guevarism, who initiated the formation of the radical parties of Palestine (Naief Hawatmeh's Democratic Front and George Habash's Popular Front), the popular revolution in South Yemen and the War of Dhofar. In comparison with most of the analyses proposed, which are almost always too ideological (obsessed with identifying errors and 'deviations'), Sanallah Ibrahim's novel (Warda) provides a better insight into the slow death of this movement, its profound aspirations for social, collective and individual liberation (with particular regard to women), and the illusion that the Kalashnikov – over-popularized in this era of modern Arab history – could become an effective antidote to the popular classes' inertia. This Arab 'foquism' has passed away, like that of Latin America.

Official Pan-Arabism promoted the blossoming of organizations operating within the whole Arab entity. Each of the professions of the middle classes, in particular, was identified with one organization of this kind that is sometimes active (Arab Lawyers, Arab Engineers, Arab Doctors, Arab Writers etc.), just as there is, at least on paper, a confederation of trades unions (Arab Workers' Union). In the 1970s and 1980s, the intensification of intra-Arab migrations (towards the oil-rich countries) certainly helped to popularize the mutual knowledge of the Arab peoples. But it did so in a general atmosphere of depoliticization and in an environment dominated by the super-reactionary practices of the Gulf States. Its effects are therefore very ambiguous. The flow of capital in the opposite direction has not had less ambiguous effects, as it mainly enriched the speculators of the Islamist movement.

Autocratic Pan-Arabism is dead. To be convinced of this, it suffices to have attended (as the writer did) some of its (funeral) 'services', which assemble each year the cohort of its 'historic leaders' – tie-wearing men currently over seventy years old on average, and closed to younger persons and women – who still feel nostalgic for the populist era, and nothing more. Its sketch of reconciliation with the Islamic movement will certainly not have the virtue of reviving the system. On the contrary, it contributes to its dilution in the new shallow illusion: that of the Islamic Nation (*al Umma al Islamiyya*).

This page of history is turned. The Arab world no longer has its own project, neither in the local states nor in that of the entire Pan-Arab entity. This is the reason why the projects thought up for it by external agents (the United States and Europe) seem able to impose their programme.

This does not mean that the objective need for a complex alternative conceived at both national and Pan-Arab levels has disappeared from people's minds. The multiplicity of initiatives in support of the Palestinian *intifadas* (the Ligan did al Tatbi – Opposition Committees for 'normalization' of relations with Israel) constitutes a glaring testimony to the accuracy of this premise. However, this solidarity – alone – does not represent a substitute for the lack of an overall vision of the status of Arabs in the world of today.

The Palestinian people's *intifada* is a struggle for national liberation, probably the major struggle of this kind in our era. It simply expresses the people's desire not to submit to the racist apartheid system imposed by Zionism. It will end only if Israel recognizes the immediate right of Palestinians to their state, or if the powers in the developed capitalist countries undergo profound changes in kind (to the extent of forcing dominant capital to renounce its strategy aimed at systematically weakening the position of the peripheral peoples – in this case, Arabs – in the global system), which will not be swiftly or easily realized.

The Israeli authority in the territories occupied since 1967 (Gaza, the West Bank, the Golan) is setting about pursuing the plan to expand Zionist colonization, thereby recognizing only the rights of Jews alone (I emphasize Jews because in the State of Israel itself, non-

Jews are not accorded equal rights, neither collective nor individual), and this constitutes the definition of the apartheid racist state. The set of measures taken to this effect include expropriating lands for new settlers, plundering water resources and jeopardizing any form of elementary economic life for Palestinians.

Initially, this system gave the impression of being capable of achieving its ends, as the Palestinian people appeared to have accepted the management of their daily activities in the occupied territories by notables and the trading bourgeoisie. The Palestine Liberation Organization (PLO), driven away from the region after the invasion of Lebanon by the Israeli army (1982), appeared not to possess any longer the means of opposing the Zionist annexation from its exile in Tunis.

The first *intifada* took place in December 1987. An apparently 'spontaneous' explosion, the *intifada* expresses the outrage of the working classes, and particularly of the most wretched social groups, confined in refugee camps. The intifada boycotts the Israeli authority by organizing systematic acts of civil disobedience. Israel reacts with the colonial brutality that defines its nature, but is unable to re-establish its efficient police force or to bolster the timid Palestinian buffer middle classes. On the other hand, the *intifada* advocates a mass return of the political forces in exile, the establishment of new forms of local organization, and the middle classes' patronage of the sustained liberation struggle. The *intifada* was an affair for youths – *Chebab al intifada* – who were initially not organized in the formal PLO networks. The four components of the PLO (Fatah, loyal to its late chief, Yasser Arafat, the DFLP and PFLP, and the Communist Party) immediately joined the *intifada* and thus won the sympathy of many of these *Chebab*. Overtaken by their slackness in previous years, despite a couple of actions credited to the Islamic Jihad, which reappeared in 1980, the Muslim Brotherhood made way for a new form of struggle embodied in Hamas, established in 1988.

Although after two years of expansion this first *intifada* appeared to lose impetus, on account of its violent suppression by Israeli armed forces and authorities (who used firearms to fight Palestinian children and closed the 'green line' to Palestinian workers, the sole breadwinners of their families, etc.), the stage was set for a United States-sponsored 'negotiation' that was crowned by the

Madrid meeting (1991) and subsequently with the so-called Oslo Peace Accords (1993) that allowed for the return of the PLO to the occupied territories and its transformation into a 'Palestinian Authority' (1994).

The Oslo Accords had imagined the transformation of the occupied territories into one or several 'Bantustans' to be definitively integrated into the Israeli territory. Without showing much imagination, the Zionists and their American and European sponsors reconstructed in detail the entire apartheid system of racist South Africa. Israel had indeed been a faithful friend of the apartheid regime, which shared with Israel the same fundamental racist vision of humanity. In this context, the Palestinian Authority was to crystallize into nothing other than a false state – like those of the Bantustans – indeed, to become the channel for transmitting Zionist order.

Back in Palestine, the PLO-based Palestinian Authority managed to establish its order, but not without some ambiguity. The Authority absorbed into its new structures most of the *Chebab* who had coordinated the *intifada*. It acquired legitimacy via the 1996 elections in which the Palestinians participated massively (80 per cent turnout) and where an overwhelming majority elected Arafat as President of this Authority. All the components of the Palestinian political spectrum (Fatah, the DFLP, PFLP, Communist Party and Hamas) showed a great sense of political maturity by refusing to be polemical during the campaign, transferring the choice of the electorate to individuals who had been loyal and efficient in the struggle, regardless of their partisan sympathies. However, the Authority had to contend with acute financial problems, since Israel controls the entire economy of the territories, which, moreover, cannot maintain direct relations with the outside world. On the other hand, the Gulf States virtually stopped offering financial assistance to the Authority, using the pretext of Palestine's sympathy with Iraq during the invasion of Kuwait in 1990. For their part, the Europeans, who had made pleasant promises, released funds for Palestine in droplets and even acquiesced in subjecting their financial transactions to Israeli control. To face up to the situation, the Authority acquired a (de facto) monopoly of commercial transactions by eliminating the unreliable local bourgeoisie and thus managed to realize resources for the survival of its embryonic state machinery.

At this juncture, we will avoid entering into facile arguments 'for' or 'against' the Authority because, in our opinion, the Palestinian Authority is in an ambiguous situation: will it accept the functions assigned to it by Israel, the United States and Europe – 'governing a Bantustan' – or side with the Palestinian people, who refuse to be thus subjugated?

According to the partisans of the Bantustan project, the overstaffed police force (some 50,000 agents or more) allegedly does not carry out the functions expected of the service – cracking down on the Palestinian people to compel them to accept their fate. At any rate, it could also be asserted that this force is not plethoric, considering the level of violence perpetrated by the Israeli armed forces with which they may be confronted, especially if members of the Palestinian Police Force refuse to suppress their people.

Financial monopolies offered a propitious opportunity for distributing prebends and facilitating the creation of a new class of nouveaux riches, wholly dependent on representatives of the Authority. Alas, it is true that Palestinian leaders can be reproached for not behaving like exemplary militants, administering public property without deriving the least profit for personal use. But then could the Authority survive without such monopolies?

It is actually because the Palestinian people are opposed to the Bantustan project that Israel decided to denounce the Oslo Accords, of which it had dictated the terms, with a view to substituting for them the use of military violence and nothing else. War criminal Ariel Sharon's provocation on the al-Aqsa Mosque in 1998 (with the support of the then Labour Party government, which provided him with tanks), the triumphant election of this same criminal as head of the Israeli government (and the collaboration of 'doves' such as Shimon Peres in the cabinet) are therefore the root causes of the second *intifada*, still in progress.

Will this second *intifada* liberate the Palestinian people from the prospect of their planned submission to the Zionist system of apartheid?

In any case, the Palestinian people now have a genuine national liberation movement with its own, specific features. It is not based on the 'single party' system; it is apparently (if not really) 'united' and homogeneous. It is composed of members who maintain their individual personalities, their visions of the future, their ideologies, their militants and even their clients, but who are able to agree to pursue the struggle together. An amorphous group of organizations, associations and NGOs provide the operational resources for this movement. Certainly, this group is a real melting pot with certain NGOs that might merely be serving as screens for speculative corruption or for the penetration of Israeli and American intelligence agencies. But it is this same nebulous group that guarantees daily survival under the dreadful conditions resulting from the military aggression by the enemy. These organizations help the schools and health centres to operate, in addition to supplying and distributing basic commodities. Should this positive role be spurned?

2 | The Mediterranean–Gulf region: some international policy problems

This chapter concentrates on international policy problems in the region, emphasizing the geo-political concepts of the European states, in order to respond to two questions: can these concepts become autonomous vis-à-vis those who direct the global strategy of the United States? And are they compatible with positive economic and social development for the Arab and Iranian world?

Any analysis of these questions obviously involves other problems – chief among them the following:

1 the global strategies of the United States and how they may evolve;
2 the future of the international system after the collapse of Soviet power;
3 the new dimension in international relations created by weapons of mass destruction;
4 the reactions of the Arab states and Iran to their external challenges, as well as their internal conflicts;
5 the whole question of 'development' in the context of the new globalization;
6 the Palestinian question and the influence of Zionism on Western political and social forces.

The strategic hegemony of the United States

Before analysing the political and strategic options of countries in the region (European states, Russia, Turkey, Arab states and Iran), it is necessary first to discuss the strategy of the United States of America, although it is outside the region, for the simple reason that it is the only country that has a real political and military strategy at the global level. The United States sees the region as one among several others in the world and it is treated as a function of its global hegemonic objectives.

The hegemonic strategy of the United States has two general aims: to prevent the constitution of a 'Eurasian' region (Europe from the Atlantic to Vladivostok) and to secure the opening of the Third World for global capitalist expansion. In any serious analysis, these two objectives have to be closely connected and complementary, although this is overlooked by the dominant discourse. The latter is in fact based on two assumptions, which are that the Third World (whose opening to capitalist expansion is of course desired by all the Triad partners in principle) is destined to be relatively marginalized in the new globalization and that, as a consequence, the structure of the world system will depend mainly on the internal relationships between the Triad, it being understood that the European Union is by itself capable of becoming a competitor that would put an end to American hegemony.

These two assumptions are wrong. The role of the Third World, both as a provider of natural resources and as industrial producer, will necessarily increase. It is often asserted, with statistics to hand, that the role of raw materials supplied by the Third World will inevitably become less important and that thus it will be increasingly 'marginal' in the world system. It is certainly true that the evolution of technology and the large mineral resources of the North American and Australian continents have temporarily reduced such inputs from the Third World. But it does not mean that the Third World is now marginal: this is simply untrue. First, because the relative drop in its supplies is due largely to the depression that has been prevailing since 1970, but if there is to be a sustained and lengthy expansion in the future its role will become decisive. It is most likely then that the competition for raw materials will become fierce once again. This is all the more likely in that resources will be scarce, not only because of the exponential growth of Western consumer waste, but also because of the new industrialization of the peripheries. Conflicts for access to these resources have in no way lost their *raison d'être*.

Furthermore, a respectable number of countries in the South will become increasingly important industrial producers, both for their internal markets and for the world market. Importers of technology and capital, they are also rival exporters, and in the future world economic balance their weight will continue to grow. It is not only a question of a few countries in eastern Asia, such as Korea, but also the gigantic China and, one day, India and the large Latin American countries. But the acceleration of capitalist expansion in the South, far from being a stabilizing factor, can give rise only to violent conflict, internal and international, because this expansion cannot absorb, in the prevailing conditions of the periphery, the vast labour reserves concentrated there. The peripheries continue to be 'storm zones'. The centres of the capitalist system therefore have to exercise their power over the peripheries, submitting their populations to a pitiless discipline rather than attempting to satisfy their aspirations. Theoretically, this domination could be exercised by one hegemonic power, or shared by the partners of the Triad (hence the term 'sharing' that appears in certain discourses).

The American establishment has very well understood that, in their pursuit of hegemony, they have three decisive advantages over their European and Japanese rivals: control over the globe's natural resources, a military monopoly and the influence of 'Anglo-Saxon' culture, which they use to express the ideological domination of capitalism. The systematic implementation of these three advantages sheds light on many aspects of US policy, particularly the efforts made by Washington to exercise military control over Middle Eastern oil, its offensive against Korea – benefiting from the 'financial crisis' of that country – as well as against China, its subtle game of aggravating the divisions in Europe – by mobilizing its unquestioning British ally – and by preventing closer ties between the European Union and Russia.

As for the plan to have global control over the planet's resources, the fact that the USA is the only world-level military power means that there can be no strong intervention in the Third World without it. Not only that, but neither Europe (excluding the former Soviet Union) nor Japan possesses the resources essential for the survival of their economies. For example, they are particularly dependent on oil from the Gulf for their energy supplies, and will be for a long time to come, even if this decreases in relative terms. By taking over military control of the region through the Gulf War, the USA demonstrated that it was perfectly aware how this can be used to pressurize its ally-rivals. In the past, Soviet power had also understood this vulnerability of Europe and Japan and some of the USSR's interventions in the Third World were aimed at reminding Europe and Japan of this, in order to make them negotiate in other fields. It is evident that these deficiencies of Europe and Japan could be compensated if there were a serious rapprochement between Europe and Russia (the 'common home'), which is why the construction of Eurasia is seen by Washington as a nightmare.

The success of European economic and social reconstruction, which has once again become a genuine competition in the world market, had led to a certain coming together between Western and Eastern Europe (including the USSR). But it was not a strong drive and always very cautious. Only de Gaulle seemed to be convinced that it might develop further. Because – it goes without saying – an eventual constitution of Eurasia, in whatever form, would create an industrial, financial and military bloc – with abundant natural resources to boot – that would make continued US hegemony impossible.

The decision to make war in the Gulf in 1990–91 was taken by Washington to nip in the bud any attempts at constituting this 'Eurasian bloc'. Europe was deliberately weakened through the USA taking control over the oil, and the fragility of European policy was made evident, as differing points of view emerged. At the same time the USSR – already in the process of disintegration – was neutralized, the old worn-out scarecrow of the 'communist danger' being substituted by the new danger 'coming from the South'. In the short run, the American counter-offensive produced the results desired by Washington.

And while the disintegration of the USSR has changed many things, it has not modified American strategy. On the contrary, it has enabled the USA to assert its hegemonic claims with even more arrogance. It is true that the chaos now reigning in the ex-USSR, as in the other Eastern European countries, and the vulnerability of their societies, subjected as they are to unbridled capitalism, have destroyed their ability to be active players on the international chessboard. These weaknesses have encouraged another vision of 'Greater Europe', based on the Latin Americanization of the Eastern European partners and the relegation of Russia to a supplier of raw materials. But who profits from such a system, even temporarily? Without doubt it is Germany, returning to its tradition of *Drang nach Osten*, which is already well in place in Poland, the Czech Republic, Hungary, Slovenia, Croatia and the Baltic countries. The future of Russia, reduced to a supplier of raw materials, is less certain and it is here that the United States has embarked on a battle, the stakes of which the Europeans do not seem to have understood. All this is to the benefit of the centrifugal forces that are tearing the European project apart: it gives Germany 'wriggle room' that its partners do not have and reinforces the separatist game of Great Britain, always trailing in the wake of the United States.

Banking on the attraction that Anglo-Saxon culture has for the countries of northern Europe, these centrifugal forces – if they manage to converge (between Great Britain and Germany) – would limit the European project to its present boundaries, those of a 'common market' as part of neoliberal globalization and thus incapable of challenging the global hegemony of the United States. Active US intervention in European affairs, dictating the terms of NATO involvement in Yugoslavia, for instance, forms part of this strategy of neutralizing its weak European rival.

America's strategic choice, in contrast to what is said by mainstream journalists, highlights the vital importance of maintaining and reinforcing a 'political climate favourable to free enterprise' in the whole Third World and it shows its acute awareness that the Third World is far from marginal. On the contrary, the US–Third World conflict is now the main one, now that the East–West conflict is over and while the intra-Western conflict is confined to economic competition that accepts the rules of the game (more or less loyally) and does not risk developing into violent political confrontation (or military conflict, which had been the case in the history of capitalism up until 1945).

The inevitable developments in this field will even aggravate the reasons for confrontation, not only because of the industrialization of the Third World, but also because medium-size powers can become militarily 'dangerous' – able to threaten the sea and air communication routes that ensure the world hegemony of the United States. It seems Iraq had already reached that stage and that this convinced the Pentagon – well before the invasion of Kuwait on 2 August 1990 – that it was necessary to destroy the military and industrial potential of that country. What is the United States going to do in the future, vis-à-vis other Third World countries (India, for example), which are potentially even more dangerous?

The central importance given by Washington to its relationships with countries in eastern Asia points to the growing role that the Third World is destined to play in the world's balance of power. We have already put forward some thoughts on this subject, calling attention to the American strategy of dismembering China. The financial crisis of south-east Asia and Korea showed the extreme brutality of the American strategy in its relationships with 'the dangerous Third World'. A minor financial crisis – France and Great Britain have each undergone a dozen equally severe crises during the post-war period – served as a pretext to try and impose a veritable breaking up of Korean industry. Those terrible Korean monopolies (what hypocrisy!) must be dismantled and opened up for penetration – by American monopolies. The United States suffers from a financial crisis (its external debt) which is far larger per head of the population than that of Korea and this has been going on for over twenty years. Can one see the IMF proposing, as a solution to this crisis, the forced sale, for example, of Boeing (which, as far as we know, is also a monopoly) to its European rival Airbus? In fact, the USA–eastern Asia war has started. And it has little to do with Huntington's 'civilization clash', although this discourse is used to mask what is really at stake. American hegemony has launched a preventive war against a possible dangerous adversary, even though it is capitalist.

The United States thus considers the Third World as still a 'storm zone', threatening the world capitalist order, of which it considers itself to be the supreme guarantor. This is why the interventions of Washington in the Third World are never-ending: there is not a single region in which the USA has not intervened through subversion, *coups d'état*, economic and financial pressure (operated through the 'international' institutions that it controls: the World Bank and the IMF) and direct or indirect military intervention. Up until now the Europeans and the Japanese have never dared take up an openly hostile stance against these interventions and have almost always gone along with them. They have never used their votes at the World Bank and the IMF to oppose Washington's will and the European Union has even aligned its African policy with that of those financial institutions.

The importance of the Third World in the American hegemonic strategy lies at the heart of a continuing military discussion about the most appropriate means of intervention (such as rapid deployment forces, management of 'low-intensity' conflicts, etc.). In this context we should remember that, after its defeat in Vietnam, American decision-making was paralysed for years by the spectre of a new 'dirty war'. With the Gulf War, the American administration extricated itself from the impasse by opting for a concept of war involving the total destruction of the adversary country and its population, even if it could not be a real threat to American security. Genocide is once more on the agenda.

In its day the USSR was constantly adjusting to the evolutions in Atlantic relationships. In a first period – the Stalin era – it limited itself to falling back on itself, concentrating on finding a response to the new nuclear weaponry. Then it thought it could defy the hegemonic power of the United States through a worldwide military deployment, mainly by sea, supported by fragile alliances here and there in the Third World, where it seemed possible. But far from convincing Europe of the uselessness of its pro-Atlantic option, this choice by the Soviet military served only to perpetuate the illusion of the threat.

As for the Middle East, with which we are particularly concerned, the military dimension of the American strategy is primordial. This is the reason why Washington is heating up the 'Iraqi threat'. True, the failure of the second Gulf War – that of 1998, which did not take place – raises the hope that Europe may refrain from rallying shamelessly to the unilateral initiatives of Washington in the future.[1] And it is good that at the Security Council, Russia and China find themselves together again, supported by all the Third World countries and many European ones (but not the British) in refusing to transform the United Nations into an office for rubber-stamping American decisions. But it is necessary to go much further and dare to think of alternative European and Arab strategies. We are far from there as yet.

The military dimension of American strategy is naturally complemented by the political choices that it maintains, when they are not themselves dictating them. The so-called peace process in Palestine, launched at Madrid and Oslo through the declarations of 1993 (Gaza and Jericho, etc.), under American auspices, has served only to reinforce the expansionist ambitions of Israel and its military power (particularly its nuclear equipment, about which the Western media are completely silent, while they harp on other threats which are, in fact, far less frightening). In spite of the crimes committed daily in the occupied territories, the government of war criminal Ariel Sharon remains the privileged ally of the Western powers in the region. The proposal for a 'common market of the Middle East', organized around Israel – a totally 'Made in the USA' project – just rounds out this strategy and at the same time eliminates the Europeans from all influence in the region. The political support for Islamic movements, in Turkey, Egypt, Algeria and elsewhere, completes their whole strategy; in fact, no one can serve their interests better, through their servile submission to the demands of globalized neoliberalism, than the dictatorships which transfer 'resistance to the West' to the so-called 'cultural' field. On all these issues there has been no sign, up until now, of Europe refusing to fit in with the American project. There have been a few weak protests, but hardly anything more. The very idea that through its economic strength Europe could impose some 'sharing' has proved an illusion.

The question is, then, whether the countries around the Mediterranean and its extensions – Europeans, Arabs, Turks, Iranians, the Horn of Africa countries – will opt for security policies differing from those which aim primarily at safeguarding American world hegemony. Reason would seem to favour such an option. But up until now Europe has shown no sign of moving in that direction. One of the reasons for its inertia is perhaps that there are differences of interest among European partners – differences at least in priorities. The Mediterranean seaboard is not so important for the industrial centres of developed capitalism as are the seaboards of the North Sea, the American north-east Atlantic and central Japan: there is no comparison in the density of their development. For the northern Europeans – Germany and Great Britain – let alone for the USA and Japan, the danger of chaos in the countries to the south of the Mediterranean is not as serious as it could be for the Italians, the Spanish and the French.

Europe and the Arab Mediterranean to the south

Until 1945, the different European powers had their own policies in the Mediterranean and they were often in conflict with each other. After the Second World War the western European states hardly had any policies at all vis-à-vis the Mediterranean and Arab states, neither as individual states nor in common – apart from the policy of alignment with the USA. Even so, Great Britain and France, which had colonial interests in the region, fought behind the scenes to maintain their respective advantages. From 1954, Great

Britain renounced these as regards Egypt and Sudan, and in 1956, after the failure of the tripartite Suez adventure, made an agonizing about-turn in its policy regarding its special influence on the countries bordering the Gulf, abandoning the area at the end of the 1960s. France, which had already been expelled from Syria in 1945, finally accepted the independence of Algeria in 1962, but it has maintained a sort of nostalgia for its influence in the Maghreb and Lebanon, encouraged by the local governing classes, at least in Morocco, Tunisia and Lebanon.

Europe, during the assembling of EC, did not develop a common policy in this area after the retreat of the colonial powers. When oil prices were readjusted, following the Israeli–Arab war of 1973, the European community awoke from its slumbers and realized that it did indeed have 'interests' in the region. But this awakening led to no important initiatives, for example, on the Palestinian problem. Europe remained, in this field as in many others, hesitant and, in the end, inconsistent.

There had been, however, some progress during the 1970s towards a greater autonomy *vis-à-vis* the United States, culminating with the 1980 summit in Venice. But this progress was not consolidated, and during the 1980s was virtually eroded. It disappeared completely with the European alignment with Washington during the Gulf crisis. So European attitudes towards future relationships between Europe and the Arab-Iranian world have to be studied country by country.

Great Britain no longer has any specific Mediterranean and Arab policy of its own. In this field, as in others, British society – as expressed through its political parties, both Conservative and Labour – opted for unconditional alignment with the United States. This was a fundamental, historical choice which surmounted temporary situations. In the Anglo-Saxon bloc of peoples (the USA, Canada, Australia, New Zealand) there is a shared and unconditional belief in the values of capitalism and the form of bourgeois democracy associated with it, but there is also a feeling of deep shared solidarity, when confronted with other cultures in the planet.

De Gaulle was the only European politician who understood that this fundamental option was in fact incompatible with an autonomous Europe, and he felt that the formal adherence of London should not be sought. This view did not prevail and today the participation of Great Britain in the European institutions considerably reinforces the submission of Europe to the demands of American strategy. The Gulf War was a perfect demonstration of this.

For different reasons, Germany does not have a specific Arab and Mediterranean policy either, and probably will not develop one in the foreseeable future. Handicapped by its division and its status, the German Federal Republic had concentrated all its efforts on economic development, accepting a low political profile while trailing along, simultaneously and ambiguously, in the wake of both the United States and the European Common Market. The reunification of Germany and its acquisition of full international sovereignty did not change its position – on the contrary, it was reinforced. The dominant political forces (conservatives, liberals and social democrats) gave priority to the expansion of German capitalism in central and eastern Europe, so that a common European strategy became relatively less important, both politically and for economic integration.

France, a country both Atlantic and Mediterranean, heir to a colonial empire and counted among the victors of the Second World War, has not really renounced its claims to great-power status, even though its economic and financial situation does fit it for such a role. During the first decade of the post-war period, successive French governments tried to preserve the country's colonial position by extravagant claims to be pro-Atlantic, anti-communist and anti-Soviet. However, they never really gained the support of Washington, as could be seen by the US attitude at the time of the tripartite aggression against Egypt in 1956. The Mediterranean and Arab policy of France was then, inevitably, retrograde.

De Gaulle broke with these illusions, which were both 'palaeo-colonial' and pro-American. He then conceived an ambitious three-fold project: to modernize the French economy, to carry out a decolonization policy and to replace its out-of-date colonialism with flexible neocolonialism, compensating for the country's inherent weakness – common to all medium-sized countries – through European integration. De Gaulle conceived of a Europe that could be autonomous vis-à-vis the United States, not only in the economic and financial fields, but also politically and even militarily. He also envisaged associating the then USSR with the construction of Europe ('Europe from the Atlantic to the Urals'). With considerable lucidity, he foresaw the gradual relaxing of the Soviet system: the 'convergence of systems'. He was not convinced that the 'demonization' of the USSR was correct, for he saw how this was used by the USA to affirm its hegemony and to subordinate a nervous western Europe. This geo-strategic conception of the construction of a Eurasia confronting the North American continent was not to the taste of Washington, as already mentioned. It would have also meant an Arab policy for France that distanced itself from the strictly military policy towards the Mediterranean and the Gulf region, as well as vis-à-vis Israel, used by the United States within the context of their global military strategy.

But Gaullism did not survive its founder and, from 1968, the French political classes, both traditional right and socialist left, have gradually returned to their previous positions. Their vision of European construction shrank to its 'common market' dimension, to the France–Federal German Republic partnership (to the point that when German reunification was achieved there was surprise and alarm in Paris) and to the pressing invitation to Great Britain to join in the EEC (not realizing that Britain would act as the Trojan horse for the Americans in Europe). Of course this slide meant that France had to abandon any Arab policy worthy of the name – in other words any policy going beyond the simple defence of immediate trade interests. In fact, French political policy in the Arab world, as in sub-Saharan Africa, has been to play a supportive role in American hegemonic strategy.

It is in this context that it has been found necessary to replace the Mediterranean discourse, which aimed at hitching the Maghreb countries on to the European waggon (as was done with Turkey – a policy now in crisis). This destroys the prospect of getting closer to the Arab states and it also means abandoning the Mashreq[2] to US/Israeli intervention. There is little doubt that the Maghreb ruling classes, by going along with this policy, are also responsible – although the Gulf crisis dealt it a serious blow, as the peoples of north Africa vigorously demonstrated their solidarity with the Mashreq, as could have been foreseen.

Italy, because of its geographical position, is obviously concerned by Mediterranean problems. This does not necessarily mean that it therefore has a genuine Mediterranean and Arab policy, and still less does it mean that it is effective or autonomous. Italy was for a long time marginalized by capitalist development and its Mediterranean ambitions had to be framed within a forced alliance with other, more decisive, European countries. From its unification in 1870 to the fall of Mussolini in 1943, it has always hesitated between allying itself with the masters of the Mediterranean – that is, Great Britain and, in second place, France, at least since the Entente Cordiale of 1904 – or with those who could contest the Anglo-French positions: in other words, Germany and, in second place, Austria-Hungary.

But the Italy of today is no longer the Italy of that period. It is considered the greatest 'miracle' of capitalist development in the centre during the post-war era. Now a fully fledged European state, it can offer its citizens a standard of living equal or superior to those of a Great Britain in decline, and it is capable of providing effective, if selective, competition on the world market. It could thus develop its own Arab policy and/or carry its weight in the European balance of power, in the sense of developing a common, autonomous policy, as opposed to falling in with American hegemonic strategies. But it has not done so up until now. Italy has not regained its sovereignty in defence and has accepted its role as the southern base of NATO without making any conditions or receiving any advantages in exchange. It has not tried to rebuild a modernized military force, as Great Britain, France and Germany have done. It has reduced its defence forces to such a strict minimum that they have no autonomous operational capability. For certain analysts this pacifist choice is one of the reasons for its extraordinary economic success. But this could be contested, as certain military expenditures play an important role in technological innovation and therefore competitivity in leading economic sectors.

As for long-term options, Italian opinion is considerably less monolithic than that in other countries. These differences can be classified as four tendencies: Atlanticism, universalism, *Mittel*-Europeanism and Mediterraneanism.

Atlanticism, which in Italy involves a low-visibility foreign policy overshadowed by the USA, has dominated the action and choices of Christian Democrat governments since 1947. It is equally dominant, in an even more ideological form, in certain sectors of the secular bourgeoisie (Republicans, Liberals, some Socialists), as the Christian Democrats are conditioned by the pressure of the Catholic tradition of universalism. It is not insignificant that the papacy has often taken up a less retrograde attitude towards the Arab peoples (particularly on the Palestinian issue) and other Third World peoples, than those of many Italian governments and Western governments in general. The leftward shift of part of the Catholic Church, under the influence of the liberation theology of Latin America, is now reinforcing this universalism, of which secular versions exist in pacifist, ecological and Third World circles.

The *Mittel*-European tendency has its roots in the Italian nineteenth century and the North/South divide that unification of the country has not overcome. Tied to the interests of big capital in Milan, it wants priority given to the economic expansion of Italy towards eastern Europe, in close association with Germany. At the moment, Croatia is an immediate target – to the extent that some analysts see it as reflecting Italian expansionist aims towards Dalmatia. Clearly this would require Italy, like Germany, to pursue its traditional international low profile and, in particular, it would marginalize its relationships with the countries on the south side of the Mediterranean. This inevitably diminishes the scope of the construction of Europe, without questioning it in a formal way. A similar option on the part of Spain – we shall return to this a bit later – would yet further isolate France in the European community, which would be reduced to the lowest common denominator.

'Mediterraneanism' remains a weak tendency in spite of the contribution that universalism could bring to it. It therefore manifests itself in a 'Levantine' manner: 'doing business' here and there, without worrying about the political framework within which it operates. If it is to gain greater consistency and be more respected, involving Italy in economic openings that aim at reinforcing its autonomy and that of its Arab partners, there will have to be a convergence between this tendency and the universalist ideals, particularly those of the Italian left, both communist and Christian.

The Italian right, reunited under the leadership of Berlusconi, has chosen to follow in the footsteps of the Atlantic axis: Washington/London/Berlin. This choice was made only too clear by the behaviour of the police during the G8 meeting in Genoa in July 2001.

Spain and Portugal play an important role in the US geo-strategy for world hegemony. Indeed the Pentagon considers the Azores/Canaries/Gibraltar/Balearic Islands axis as essential for monitoring the north and south Atlantic and the narrow entrance to the Mediterranean. Thus the USA created an alliance with these two countries just after the Second World War, evincing little compunction about dealing with their fascist governments. On the contrary, the frenzied anti-communism of the Salazar and Franco dictatorships served the hegemonic aims of the USA very well. Portugal thus became a member of NATO and large American military bases were established on Spanish soil. In exchange, the USA and its European allies unconditionally supported Portugal in its colonial war until it was defeated.

The democratic evolution of Spain after Franco's death did not challenge the integration of the country into the American military system. On the contrary, the formal adherence of Spain to NATO (in May 1982) was even the subject of an electoral blackmail, giving the impression that participation in the EEC required NATO membership, which a majority of public opinion did not want. Since then Madrid has unreservedly aligned itself with the positions of Washington. In exchange, the USA has, it seems, intervened to 'moderate' the Moroccan claims on Ceuta and Melilla and even tried to influence Great Britain on Gibraltar, although there is some doubt about the latter case.

The reinforced Atlantic alignment of Madrid has brought about radical changes in the organization of the Spanish armed forces, which have been described by analysts as a 'shift to the south'. Traditionally, the Spanish army was distributed all over the territory. It was also seen – and, since Franco took power, in a very evident way – as more of an internal police than a strike force against an external enemy. The Spanish army had in fact remained rustic, and in spite of the marked attentions given by the top political authorities in Madrid to the generals and other officers, it never underwent a real modernization, as did the armies of France, Great Britain and Germany.

The socialist governments and afterwards the right then proceeded to redeploy the Spanish forces to form a possible 'southern front' and, at the same time, they started modernizing the army, the air force and the navy. This 'shift to the south', which was demanded by Washington and NATO, is one of many signs of the new American domination strategy, replacing the east with the south in the 'defence' of the West.

In Spain this shift is accompanied by a new discourse, stressing the 'hypothetical enemy coming from the south', whose identity, ambiguous and vague as it is, leaves little in doubt. Oddly enough, this discourse among the Spanish democrats (and socialists) draws on the old tradition of the Reconquest, popular among Catholic circles in the army. The shifting of the Spanish armed forces thus implies the determination of Spain to play an active role within NATO in the context of the reorientation of Western strategies, in anticipation of strong-arm intervention in the Third World. The Iberian peninsula is already the first base of the Washington/Tel Aviv axis, at the head of the main European bridge of the American Rapid Deployment Force (which played a decisive role in the Gulf War), completed by the bases in Sicily (which, also, have served only for operations against the Arab world: Libya, the Israeli bombing of Tunisia, etc.) and, strangely enough, the facilities accorded by Morocco. It is clear that this Western option robs the 'Euro-Arab' discourse of any serious content. The new democratic Spain, which claims to have a friendly policy towards Latin America and the Arab world, has, in fact, moved in the opposite direction from its declarations of principle.

Madrid, bolstered by its unconditional pro-Atlantic stance, hoped that this would pay off, at least in terms of prestige. But here Spain came up against the traditional reservations of Portugal, which rejected Madrid's proposals to constitute a unified Iberian command. As for the modernization of the army, it has been delayed by the backwardness of Spanish technology, the responsible experts considering that the present state of the country prevents it from mastering the technology appropriate for its military responsibilities. This is why, in the meantime, the USA has taken on direct responsibility for controlling the strategic Canaries/Gibraltar/Balearic Islands axis.

Spain did not, under Aznar, choose to rally to the camp of those, within the European framework, who desired autonomy vis-à-vis the United States. Aznar's right-wing government confirmed Madrid's pro-Atlantic strategy. Even more than Italy, Spain refused to capitalize on its Mediterranean position to promote a new European policy towards the Arab, African and Third Worlds: it distanced itself from the idea because of the requirements of American hegemony. The French suggestion of a Mediterranean group within the European Union remained suspended, without any serious support. Also in the economic field, Spanish capital, which has inherited the Franco legacy, is pinning its main hopes of expansion on making agreements with Germany and Japan, inviting them to participate in the modernization of Catalonia.[3]

As long as the East–West confrontation existed, the demarcation line passed through the Balkans. When the countries of the region were forced to align with Moscow or Washington – the only exception being Yugoslavia since 1948, then Albania as from 1960 – local nationalist quarrels were forced underground. This turned the Balkans into a powder keg.

From 1945 onwards, Turkey decided to be in the Western camp, after quickly ending its neutrality, which had been rather well disposed to Hitler's Germany. The Soviet claims on Kars and Ardahan in the Caucasus and the right of passage in the Dardanelles, which were put forward by Stalin right after the victory, could be rejected by Ankara only with the strong support of Washington. In exchange, Turkey, which was also a member of NATO in spite of its undemocratic policies, received American bases, which became the closest ones to Russia. Nevertheless, Turkey remained a Third World society, even if, since Ataturk, the governing elite proclaims the 'Europeanness' of the new Turkey, as it knocks on the door of the European Union, which seems reluctant to accept it. As a faithful ally of the USA and its European partners in the Gulf War, does Turkey want to return to its roots and play an active role in the Middle East, making the West pay for any services it could render them in this region? The handicap of the Kurdish question, the existence of which it refuses to acknowledge, has apparently made Turkey hesitate up until now. The same goes for an eventual option for Pan-Turanianism,[4] proposed just after the First World War in certain Kemalist circles and later relegated to the history museum. But now the dissolution of the former USSR could encourage Ankara to go for a turcophone bloc which, from Azerbaijan to Sinkiang, would dominate central Asia. Iran has always been nervous of such a development, which would not only challenge the status of southern Iranian Azerbaijan, but also the security of its long northern frontier with Turkmenistan and Uzbekistan.

Greece did not join the anti-Soviet camp of its own accord. It was forced to do so by British intervention, supported by the USA. In accordance with the Yalta Agreement, the Soviet Union abandoned the Greek resistance. This was led by the Communist Party, which had liberated the country, as it had done in Yugoslavia and Albania, and because of this was supported by a large popular majority. Against this popular movement, the West thus supported successive repressive regimes, leading finally to dictatorship by fascist colonels, ignoring the flagrant contradiction with their discourse, according to which NATO protected 'the free world' against the totalitarian 'Satan'. When democracy returned to Greece through the victory of Pasok in 1981, there was thus a risk of the country's loyalty to NATO being challenged. The European Community then came to the help of Washington in difficulty by – as was done with Spain – linking the Greek candidature to the EEC to the maintenance of its participation in the Atlantic alliance. But the integration of the country into the EEC was in fact the subject of vigorous debate among Greek public opinion at that time.

The decision of Papandreou to rally nevertheless to the Atlantic alliance, after some hesitations and in spite of the Third World and neutral principles of Pasok, seems to have set in motion an irreversible evolution in the mentalities of the Greek people, encouraging their aspirations to modernity and Europeanness. However, their new European partners had not much to offer to the country, destined to remain for a long time the poor relation in the construction of Europe.

The loyalty of Athens to the Euro-American West was not repaid either by any real support for Greece in its conflict with Turkey. There is no doubt that, in this complex conflict, often dominated by the emotions created by history, the validity of the causes, in terms of democracy, is often arguable. The lot of the Turkish minority in Thrace is hardly to be envied, while the Greek claim of exclusive rights over the wealth of the Aegean Sea, in terms of legal rights and equity, is equally arguable. Nevertheless, while the Greek dictatorship had a certain responsibility for the Cypriot tragedy of 1974, the open Turkish aggression (Operation Attila) and the subsequent creation of a 'Turkish Republic of Cyprus', violating the status of the island, were not only accepted, but probably prepared in agreement with the Pentagon. Once again, Europe acquiesced. It is clear that, for the United States, the friendship of Turkey, a considerable regional military power, takes precedence over that of Greece, even if that country is now democratic.

The whole Balkan-Danubian region (Yugoslavia, Albania, Hungary, Romania and Bulgaria) fell into the lap of Moscow because of the Soviet military occupation and the agreements made at Yalta, but also because of their own liberation and the choice of the people in Yugoslavia and Albania.

Titoist Yugoslavia, isolated from 1948 to 1953 because it was ostracized by both Moscow and Western anti-communism, followed a successful policy of creating a 'non-aligned' front, which earned it the friendship of the Third World, particularly after the Conference of Bandung in 1955. Yugoslav geo-strategic analysts at the time noted the curious fact that this policy did not seriously take into account the Mediterranean aspect of their country. This 'historical oversight' is perhaps due to Italy having abandoned, after the Second World War, its traditional aspirations to Dalmatia (and Albania) and the solution reached in 1954 on the thorny question of Trieste. Since then Yugoslavia, as a state, had been concerned mainly with balancing its relationships in the Balkan-Danubian region and above all with the balance of power between the superpowers. Regarding the former, Yugoslavia managed to capitalize, for its own benefit, on both the northern and Danubian attraction of Croatia-Slovenia and the Russian and Balkan attraction of Serbia.

The more flexible approach initiated by Khrushchev and continued by his successors as they recognized the positive role of Titoist neutralism on the world scene, as well as a softening of the regimes of the Warsaw Pact as from 1960 and especially after 1970: all these developments had guaranteed the security of Yugoslavia, which no longer felt it was the object of any regional conflict. Yugoslav diplomacy could then be exercised in the international field, which gave the country a weight out of all proportion to its size.

However, while this diplomacy certainly has had some successes in Asia, Africa and even in Latin America, it made no headway in Europe, where its calls for broadening the neutralist front never met with a favourable reaction. And yet, confronted by NATO Europe, from the north to the south of the continent and between two antagonistic military pacts, Sweden, Finland and Austria could have envisaged common positive initiatives, distancing themselves from Cold War attitudes. Later, in 1982, Greece under the leadership of Pasok tried to broaden this European neutralist camp, when it proposed cooperation with a view to the denuclearization of the Balkans and approaching certain countries from one of the two alliances (Turkey, Romania and Bulgaria), as well as the neutral ones (Yugoslavia and Albania). These proposals received no response.

The disintegration of south-eastern Europe from 1989 onwards completely changed the situation. The erosion and then the collapse of legitimacy of the region's regimes – which were based on a certain degree of development, although they had their limits and negative aspects – had shattered the unity of the ruling class. Parts of them, in desperation, tried to recast their legitimacy on the basis of nationalism. Thus conditions were ripe for an offensive by unbridled capitalism, supported by the United States and the European Union. These conditions also allowed Germany to regain its initiative in the region through its hasty recognition of Slovenian and Croatian independence, endorsed by the European Union. All this threw oil on the fire and accelerated the break-up of Yugoslavia and the outbreak of civil war. Curiously, the Europeans tried to impose on Bosnia the coexistence of communities which they had been preaching should be separated elsewhere! For, if it were possible for Serbs, Croats and Muslims to coexist in that little Yugoslavia which was Bosnia, why could they not coexist in the large Yugoslavia? Obviously such a strategy had no chance of success, which enabled the United States, in turn, to intervene in the heart of Europe. According to Washington strategy, the Balkans/Caucasus/central Asia axis is in fact an extension of the Middle East. Thanks to their exclusive control over the region, facilitated by the Gulf and Yugoslav wars, the United States has gained control over most of the oil resources of the planet.

From the above analyses concerning the political and strategic options of the countries lying to the north of the Mediterranean, one main conclusion can be drawn: most of these countries (France, Italy, Spain, Portugal, Greece and Turkey), which used to be faithful partners of the United States in the East–West conflict, have remained aligned with the strategy of American hegemony as concerns the Third World as well as, oddly enough, the Arab countries and the other countries in the Red Sea/Gulf region. The others (Balkan and Danubian countries), which were once involved in one way or another in the East–West conflict, have ceased to be active agents in the permanent North–South conflict, and have become the passive objects of Western expansionism.

After the Soviet collapse and the Gulf and Yugoslav wars

The post-Second World War period is definitively over and the collapse of Soviet power is the most evident demonstration of this. Are we going to see, then, a recomposition of the integrated world system and, on this basis, new growth, more or less generalized, even if it must necessarily be unequal? The discourse of the powers and ideologies that dominate the West would point to this as the only prospect. They are unable to assess the obstacles in any other way than being only 'temporary' (although the explosive and growing internal contradictions make this unlikely). Furthermore, the wars in the Gulf and Yugoslavia caused a media explosion attributing further virtues to this prospect, which would open up the way to a reconstruction of the world system based on 'law' (!) and 'justice' (!!), guarantee of a long peace, etc.

The attempt to reunify the world through the market is a reactionary utopia because capitalist expansion, by its nature, polarizes at the world level and this polarization is unacceptable for the peoples of the periphery – most of humanity. We should remember that the twenty or thirty years of market capitalism under British hegemony (1850–80) were followed by sixty-five years of inter-imperialist rivalries and, from 1917 onwards, by seventy years of delinking by Russia and then by China. The unification of the world through the market and hegemony, far from being the rule in the history of actually existing capitalism, has been a fragile phenomenon, lasting only briefly. The law of the system is sustainable rivalry and delinkages. It is thus arguable that the 'new equilibrium' will inevitably increase polarization, although in new ways (the semi-industrialized countries of the Third World – and those of the former East Europe – forming the new periphery in tomorrow's world); that the liberal ideology is incapable of addressing the problem of development properly; and that a strategy of delinking, which implies a polycentric world, cannot be avoided.

As for the mid-term prospects concerning the European region and the Arab and Iranian world, it is more useful to pose the problem the other way round – in other words, what 'should' be the 'ideal' relations between these regions – in order to see what has to be done to attain this objective. We can then see that recent events have not prepared the ground for a more favourable development but, on the contrary, have created more obstacles along the way. This can be seen from the increasing turbulence in the world, which does not, even chaotically, fit into the designs for desired reconstruction but, on the contrary, aggravates the contradictions of the system.

The 'ideal' model presupposes, of course, a system of values underpinning it. The criteria would be: reducing the development gap between the partners (western Europe, eastern Europe, Russia, the semi-industrialized poor Arab countries, the lightly populated and financially rich oil countries, the Fourth World), an acceptable amount of national autonomy which would facilitate the elaboration of policies appropriate to the specific problems of these very different countries, progressive policies which would address essential social problems and, in this context, adjust to the opening both to the other partners and to the other regions of the world. It goes without saying that to achieve this 'ideal' would necessitate profound changes in the structures of power and the substituting of new social hegemonies for those that today define these powers. These substitutions could be spelt out as follows: the construction of a world 'wage' hegemony, instead of that of European Western capital; the construction of a popular social alliance to replace unbridled capitalism in the East; the construction of popular national alliances instead of comprador hegemonies in the Arab world, Iran and Turkey. All this gives an idea of the immense tasks which still have to be accomplished to make such a prospect possible, as the active social and political subjects who could take action in this way exist only as potential forces, because the political organizations and dominant ideological expressions have no hold on the real issues of the ongoing conflicts.

If we can imagine the obstacles to these changes having been overcome, the 'ideal' model then clearly presupposes the consolidation of these regions (Europe, the Arab world, Turkey and Iran) and the organizing of their interdependent relationships so as to support their development along the progressive and democratic lines described above. The structure of such regional consolidation and the obstacles that they have to overcome should once again be emphasized. 'European integration' is more than desirable, it is necessary – but it should certainly not follow the model of the present European Union (liberal integration of the market without any common progressive social and political dimensions) and this, whether the union is limited to its present numbers or gradually enlarged towards the east. The concept of a 'common home', even if it is vague, corresponds better to our vision because it presupposes a margin of relative autonomy which would enable the less competitive partners to adopt specific policies. This would not exclude greater integration of the smaller group of more advanced countries, as long as they take on a progressive social policy (hegemony of the wage-earning world), which is absent from the European Union as it is at present. The construction of an Arab entity would be the necessary Southern counterpart in the ideal model, if only for the reason – obvious and so often repeated – that the Arab countries, as they are at present, are not able to take on the challenges of modern development. In a progressive vision of a common future in the serious sense of the term, Europeans and Arabs must accept their mutual reinforcement by strengthening their respective regional entities and cease looking at them as 'dangers'.

The recent past has certainly reinforced all the negative aspects of the centre–periphery polarization that is inherent in 'actually existing capitalism': the growing gap between Europe, the countries of the Third World and those of the Fourth World; the consolidation of balkanization and increased vulnerability of the countries of the region; the reinforcement of the internal social inequalities in almost all countries; the impasse of democracy, etc. It is still more serious that the dominant political and ideological forces in the European partners – among the left as well as the right – do not see that Arab unity might be desirable. Europe has not got rid of its traditional imperialist attitude, which sees 'the Other' – above all if this Other is culturally different – as an enemy that must be kept weak and divided. The world order of actually existing capitalism is based on this fundamental principle and there is no indication that Western opinion is able to renounce it.

For the last half-century, this unbridled capitalism has had only one strategic aim in the Middle East: to perpetuate what is euphemistically called the accessibility of oil but which is in fact the domination of the Western powers over this wealth, the exploitation of which must be used for the economic expansion of the West exclusively. There are two complementary ways of attaining this objective. One is to perpetuate the division of the Arab world and ensure the survival of the archaic regimes in the Gulf – Saudi Arabia, Kuwait, the Arab Emirates – so as to destroy any possibility that oil wealth may be put at the service of the Arab peoples. The other is to guarantee the absolute military supremacy of Israel, which has been given nuclear arms so that it can intervene at any time. The Gulf War showed that Europe had no conception of its relationships with the Arab world, which was not the case of the United States. The permanent blackmail of Israel, forcing the West as a whole to show solidarity against the 'barbarians' of the East, forms part of this strategy and is effective only because Europe does not have its own vision of its relations with the countries to the south of it, Arab, Turk and Iranian.

The different mid-term scenarios concerning the North–South relationships for this region can now be reviewed in light of the above considerations. The main, distinguishing factor is always, when it comes down to it, the degree of autonomy that Europe has vis-à-vis the United States and the extent of regionalization within the world system that can accompany it.

The scenario of a collective European neo-imperialism that has special domination over 'its' Arab and African South does perhaps comfort those who are nostalgic for the past, but the Gulf War showed that it was inconsistent. If oil has to be controlled by 'the West' this can be done directly only by the American army and Europe can only play the card of friendship with the Arab peoples against this project. The Arab world does not belong to the sphere of influence of the European Union, but to that of the United States, in the same way that southern Africa will probably be reorganized around South Africa in the future. The only real European sphere may be the African Fourth World. Germany, in fact, seems to realize this and acts accordingly. As for Russia, it is still far from being capable of making its presence felt externally. In the mid-term, Europe does not exist; it is a political lightweight.

Must one then speak of the restoration of US hegemony, which has been too quickly dismissed? Something quite different is surely emerging: a trio, US–Japan–Germany, in which the roles and prospects are different. Japan and Germany will push their advantage in economic rivalry, while the USA will fulfil the role – costly for it in terms of economic competition – of the policeman whose responsibility it is to maintain this very special world order. This order, which seems to be the mid-term prospect, can be termed 'the Empire of Chaos'. It is not in fact the construction of a new world order a little less bad than the previous one (the post-Second World

War period), but a kind of military world order to accompany the neoliberal order of unbridled capitalism.

In the global strategy of Washington, the functions given to the European armies are those of auxiliaries whose job it is to occupy the territory prepared by high-altitude bombing. The United States reserves decision-making for itself, as of course it reserves the power to make the final political decisions within NATO.

Notes

1 In spite of the first resolution of the Security Council, which did not allow the war, the USA went ahead with it anyway. Subsequent resolutions give a veneer of legitimacy to the action, but do little to legitimize the occupation of Iraq.

2 Mashreq means the Levant, or the East, and it refers to all the Arab countries east of (and including) Egypt. Maghreb (literally 'the setting sun') refers to the Arab countries to the west of Egypt.

3 Some time later, Aznar was defeated in an election precisely because the vast majority of Spaniards had condemned the war.

4 'Pan-Turanianism' is the drive towards union of peoples speaking the Turanian or Ural-Altaic languages.

3 | Euro-Mediterranean relationships: globalization and regionalization

It is Eric Hobsbawm to whom we turn when asking ourselves what, in light of recent events, is going on in the world. For he has captured better than anyone the turbulent, often tragic activities of capitalism, in his excellent, dense work, *The Age of Extremes*, which starts with the First World War and ends with the fall of the Berlin Wall in 1989.[1] But we also turn to Samir Amin who, as an observer of our contemporary world, relentlessly criticizes the illusions promoted by this capitalism and warns us of the latest illusions, those of 'globalization' – the new era which will make a 'global village' of our planet.

People often used to laugh at the naïveté of socialist propaganda when it proclaimed the 'radiant dawn' of the future. But they forget that this belief in 'progress', typical of modern times, lies also at the heart of the capitalist adventure. It has often been belied by history, but it is constantly renewed by tame intellectuals whose job it is to announce the glorious future to those who, understandably enough, have their doubts.[2]

We should recall the appalling era of colonization, which the conquerors presented as a modernization of traditional societies, or the no less terrible era of decolonization and the enormous sacrifices needed to leave it behind. Two so-called 'world' wars caused millions of deaths and gave rise to means of massive destruction such as the nuclear bomb. Far from appearing as the monstrous effects of the conflicts of interest generated by capitalism, these were presented, in their turn, as the struggle of Good against Evil. And this very convenient myth was rapidly employed once again to justify the Cold War and the billions of dollars spent on nuclear armaments. As it was used later to cover up the sordid interests of the Gulf War and the more recent Balkan war.

At the beginning of the third millennium, this belief or system of beliefs, developed and expanded by the new means of communication and information, is called 'globalization'.[3] This is not the place to dwell on the tremendous barrage of the media, which ranges from scholarly debates to forums like that of Davos, from the economic and mathematical justifications of the exceptionally gifted experts of the World Bank or the International Monetary Fund to 'popular' best-sellers like *The End of History* of Fukuyama or the *Clash of Civilizations* of Huntington. But we should bear in mind the prodigious measures used to legitimize, at the world level, this new cycle of capitalism. The stakes are enormous.

Let us look at some of its main characteristics.

Capitalism as a system of production is not new, nor is its development at the international level. 'The Great Transformation', to use Karl Polanyi's phrase,[4] began several centuries ago and it has not finished its work of submitting all forms of social life to the profit motive. It has been marked by economic and social crises, bloody conflicts, massive destruction of entire populations and cultures, but it has continued its homogenizing action, spreading to all continents and all spheres of human activity. It is 'totalitarian' by definition because its logic excludes all other logic. But its 'totalitarianism' is far from being uniform and there are many and varied resistances, from the most conservative, such as ethnic and religious identity, to the more innovatory, such as the Attac movement.

The most important and best organized resistance was that of 'actually existing socialism' which forced capitalism to 'humanize' its action throughout the twentieth century. Keynesianism, the welfare state, Fordism, developmentalism were in large part made possible by the existence of a strong, organized alternative to pure capitalism.[5]

With the collapse of the 'socialist camp' which all the media images showing the fall of the Berlin Wall have transformed into the founding event of a new epoch, the 'end of history' was announced and, for a temporarily victorious capitalism, the constraints imposed by competition between the two systems no longer counted. 'Liberalism', finally liberated from its socialist alter ego, shook off its social and political encumbrances and became 'neoliberal' – in other words openly and entirely liberal. It is the time of 'deregulation', exclusive market-oriented laws to organize not only production, but also culture, education, health, the relations between states and societies, between nations and corporations, between generations, etc.

This trend, of course, started well before 1989, but at the beginning it affected only the less resistant Western societies like the United

States of America under Reagan and Great Britain under Thatcher, or the weakest nation-states of Africa and Latin America through the Structural Adjustment Programmes (SAPs).

The barrier created by the socialist alternative having disappeared and discretion no longer being necessary, the contemporary form of capitalism, neoliberalism, thus becomes today's hegemonic way of thinking and the liberation of market forces the ultimate aim of 'good governance'. This strategic victory coincides with a profound change in the production system, especially in the field of communication and information. As Manuel Castells has observed:[6]

> The new information technologies, by transforming the process of information treatment, influence all spheres of human activities and make it possible to establish innumerable connections between different fields, as well as between the elements and agents of these activities. Thus a network economy emerged, which was extremely interdependent and which became increasingly able to apply the progress of its technology, knowledge and management to technology, knowledge and management themselves. [...] This new economy is informational because the productivity and competitiveness of its units essentially depends on their capacity to apply effective information based on knowledge [...] this new economy is global because the key activities of production, consumption and distribution, as well as their constituents (capital, labour, primary materials, management, information, technology, markets) are organized at the world level, either directly or through a network of contacts between the economic agents.

The strategic victory of capitalism and the information revolution thus combine to accelerate the globalization movement 'inserting economic activities all over the world into an interdependent system that functions as a unit in real time'.[7]

Capitalism is thus a winner twice over. First, at the strategic level: with the collapse of the competing experience of 'actually existing socialism', the dominant classes are freed from the political, social and even ethical restraints they had ended by adopting as a philosophy: the old bourgeois humanism of the nation-state, European-style, with the regulation of public policies, as well as the

Keynesian regulation of the economy. Second, at the technological level: with the constraints of space–time breaking down, one after the other, it became possible to manage globalized economic units (production, trade, finance) in real time.

The whole new ideology of globalization rests on this double success. Cleverly playing on these two keyboards, the fantastic successes of the new technologies and the lamentable failure of the socialist experience, the 'new evangelists of the market' proclaim on high that the path thus opened up is unique, irrefutable; that it is to the laws of the market and profit that we owe thanks for this progress and therefore by extending them to all societies and all aspects of social activity, humanity can progress. That this new capitalist ideology effectively 'gives new life' to capitalism, by presenting it as a system of production, which is new, global (or becoming so), inevitable and unavoidable. Like all ideology closed up within its dogmas, it prohibits any alternative thinking, dismissed in advance as being conservative and reactionary.

Backed by the powerful Bretton Woods institutions, taking full advantage of the most modern communication and information techniques, its job is to provide a universal legitimacy for what, after all, is but the result of a specific history and, as such, is susceptible to change.

Globalization and regionalization

The new developments help us to understand the present dynamic of the capitalist system and we have used these insights to try to analyse the efforts being made to create a 'Euro-Mediterranean' space.

We should first remember that the nation-state as a socio-historical form of capitalist development is not 'in itself' exclusive of other forms, local, regional or transnational. Merchant capitalism existed in the oldest empires, in China, India and the Middle East.[8] But it is in Europe that capitalism, driven by the first Industrial Revolution, was to take real root in production activities and become the leading mode of production. At the same time, new kinds of states appear on the scene, which shaped, in different forms, the social milieu in order to make 'nations': England, France, Germany and, later on, the countries to the south and east of Europe.

These capitalist nation-states such as England and France possessed a far-flung collection of colonies and were already global capitalist systems. The first of them developed with the British Industrial Revolution and it affected all Europe and then the United States, before the cycle was closed with Russia and Japan. Western Europe governed the world, but there were rivalries between European countries and these exploded in 1914 in what is known as the First World War.

The post-war period was unstable. It saw the rise of the USA and its 'challenger' the USSR, but also the increasing power of the last capitalist nation-states, Germany and Japan. All this ended by the gigantic explosion of the Second World War, which was succeeded by the Cold War, a period of structural competition between the two systems. It accelerated decolonization but it also changed imperialism: the territorial possessions lost out to more cunning forms of domination, such as economic and technological 'dependence'.

With the end of the Cold War, the primacy of the United States was evident and the new system that has developed could be termed 'more capitalist than ever', but also more 'American'. Accumulation takes place at unequal levels. It is aided by the elimination of customs duties that the WTO (World Trade Organization) expects to complete within a few decades, the deregulation of the economy in the different nation-states as well as the liberalization of financial flows, but also by the information revolution, which provides it with a technological base that is extraordinarily effective.

At the same time, however, there has been a structural change in the economy, with an increasing number of multinationals or, more precisely, 'transnationals' that operate in networks.[9] The multiplication and concentration of these corporations in certain sectors over the last few decades are among the main characteristics of contemporary capitalism. They have helped to accelerate the exchanges in commodities and are now responsible for 60 per cent of world trade. It is estimated that they account for some 30 per cent of production. They have been helped by the large banks and financial institutions such as the International Monetary Fund, the World Bank and the World Trade Organization, which have attacked the old forms of state regulation, their main target. In this way they have directed much of the capital flow towards short-term investment (hot money), weakening the framework of monetary creation by the central banks and thus promoting the stock market crashes that, within days, can bring down whole national economies.

The structure of the world economy becomes unstable, while it weakens state forms of intervention in the fields of taxes, banking, customs and stock markets.

In the new system, however, the unequal development between classes, countries and regions is destined to worsen. The general freeing up of trade and financial transactions enfeebles all national institutions, beginning with those of the weaker countries. Certain countries, Korea, Malaysia and China, have been resisting, or are organizing themselves regionally, but most of them are trying to accelerate the 'reforms' (concerning taxes, banking and social affairs) which are supposed to promote general growth but in fact mainly benefit the new neoliberal credo.

Since 1990 there has been a geographical polarization which has taken the form of regional bodies that go beyond national frontiers. But the most active regionalizations have been those forged around the central poles of the world economy, the Triad: Japan and south-east Asia, the United States of America, western Europe.

The European Union is the oldest of these regional constructions. Launched by the Treaty of Rome in 1957, the European Economic Community (EEC) was then composed of only six countries and grew out of former organizations, created just after the Second World War, such as the Organization for European Co-operation and Development (OECD) and the European Coal and Steel Community (ECSC). Their aims were to reconstruct a Europe that had been ruined by the war, to calm French–German conflicts and, under the leadership of NATO, to constitute a front vis-à-vis the countries of Eastern Europe.

The EEC increased its forms of cooperation in order to ensure the independence of the region in the fields of energy and, especially, agriculture, with the Common Agricultural Policy (CAP). The regionalization movement gathered momentum, spreading to other sectors, and then, in 1986, the Single Act was signed, which envisaged the removal of internal frontiers and the free circulation of people, goods and capital. In 1992, the Treaty of Maastricht envisaged the relaunching of the political union but also the construction of an economic and monetary union, with the establishment of a European Central Bank by 1997 at latest. And, while the regionalization movement consolidated the European Union (now with fifteen members), there emerged NAFTA, formed round the USA, and ASEAN, formed round Japan.

As this regionalization process took place in an avowedly neo-liberal framework, it weakened the traditional means of regulation of nation-states without, however, transferring their powers to a regional regulating authority. Brussels has remained a soulless bureaucratic apparatus, strongly influenced by the Bretton Woods institutions and by policies for freeing up the market. Unemployment, the job crisis, deregulation of the economy, the reductions in non-productive expenditure (health, education, etc.) were the results of the famous 'Maastricht criteria' which were but the European velvet glove covering the iron hand of world neoliberalism.

As Pierre Bourdieu has remarked:[10]

> What is at issue is the role of the state (both the national state as it now exists and the European state that is to be created), particularly as concerns social rights and the role of the social state, which is the only force able to act as a counterweight to the inexorable results of the market economy when left to itself. One can be against a Europe like that of Mr Tietmeyer, which will serve the interests of the financial markets, while at the same time be in favour of a Europe which, by mutually agreed policies, can impede the violence of those markets. But there is little hope of this happening in the Europe that the bankers are preparing for us. One cannot expect that social integration will be ensured through monetary integration. On the contrary: we know that the countries that want to preserve their competitiveness within the euro area to the detriment of their partners will have no other choice but to lower their wage expenditure by reducing social charges. Social and wage dumping and the 'flexibility' of the job market will be the only choices left open to countries, as they have lost their right to interfere with the rates of exchange […] Only a European social state will be able to counteract the disintegrating effect of the monetary economy. But Mr Tietmeyer and the neoliberals do not want national states, which they consider just an obstacle to the free working of the economy, or – still less – a supranational state, which they would like to reduce to a bank.

This long quotation from one of the most perceptive social observers of this Europe in the process of creation clearly shows the ambiguity of the regionalization processes at work in the world today. It is a response as well as a reaction to the acceleration of a polarizing globalization in the precise sense of the term given it by Samir Amin.[11] These processes could follow the neoliberal logic of this polarizing globalization – or they could resist it. It will depend on the forms of action and alternatives that the social struggles in these regions will be developing in the future.

While the interests of the European popular classes are being constantly threatened by the form that the construction of Europe is taking and while, therefore, the future of this region will depend on the extent to which the social movements and intellectuals take part in this construction, what about the interests of the peoples of the less developed countries, who are the most vulnerable? You can bet that it is not Mr Tietmeyer who is going to take pity on their fate.

We should remember that, at the gates of the European Union, to the south of the Mediterranean, there are countries with fast population growth that have provided Europe, during the 'Thirty Glorious Years' (mid-1940s to mid-1970s), with the workers it needed. Now job opportunities for them are closing up in Europe, while in their own countries, Structural Adjustment Programmes have already produced their quota of unemployment, under-employment and pauperization. The question of control over the European frontiers vis-à-vis the southern side of the Mediterranean – but also eastern Europe and the Balkans – is thus a central issue in the construction of the European Union. The Mediterranean is becoming one of the most sensitive frontiers of our time.[12]

This issue shows up a major contradiction in neoliberal philosophy, which preaches the freedom of movement for goods and capital in all their forms, while prohibiting freedom of movement for people. With the polarized, unequal development that this logic will certainly accentuate where it already exists and which will be constantly stimulated when considered necessary, we can only expect huge and 'uncontrollable'[13] migratory movements throughout the world, particularly from the southern side of the Mediterranean. The construction of the European Union is – and will always be – torn by this contradiction inherent in its own logic, as indeed is the case with the United States vis-à-vis NAFTA.

The Euro-Mediterranean partnership project should also be seen in this perspective, although it should not be reduced to this dimension alone. For it reveals, in spite of all the diplomatic euphemisms and solemn declarations, a duplicity, or at least an ambiguity, that is cunningly concealed in the discourse. It is our view that this project is principally a 'defence' agreement and one that protects the EU against possible social, political and cultural 'overflowing' from the countries on the southern side of the Mediterranean. As to the presentation of the project, which is nothing if not byzantine, it merely reflects a more 'civilized' European style, compared with the brutality of the American approach to the subject. But we get the impression that the objectives are the same.

The Euro-Mediterranean partnership: fiction and fact

The process launched by the Barcelona Conference of 1995, which brings the European countries together with those on the southern side of the Mediterranean, aims at creating a free trade area, the Mediterranean Free Trade Zone (MFTZ) like the one created in North America, consisting of the USA, Canada and Mexico (NAFTA) or the one in Asia (ASEAN). As will be seen later, this initiative clearly reflects the new dynamics of globalization and is scarcely any more original, at least in its economic aims, than other such efforts.

What makes the process significant, however, are the historic and strategic conditions in which it is taking place: the Israel–Palestine and Israel–Arab conflicts and the huge migratory flows from the south to the north of the Mediterranean. These conditions obviously determine the political and institutional forms that the Europeans, who conceived the project, have adopted in order to carry it out. Our investigations therefore start with them, because of the importance given to the 'discourse' and institutions that have been set up to make the whole process permanent. The discourse is above all rhetorical, as can be seen from the following example.

The Euro-Mediterranean partnership, which came into being during the conference of the ministers of foreign affairs of the Euro-Mediterranean countries, held in November 1995 in Lisbon, constitutes the most important initiative that has been taken in modern times to develop sustainable and solid ties between both sides of the Mediterranean.[14]

Those concerned with the present relationships between the European countries and those of the southern side of the Mediterranean must surely gag at the incredible verbosity of the discourse. There has been a large number of reports, studies, reviews, colloquies and other forums in connection with meetings of more or less importance, which have taken place at more or less regular intervals. But they have always been given far more attention in the media than was warranted by their achievements on the ground, as we shall see later.

This experience has been over-emphasized because it has been deliberately publicized. It has talked too much about itself, using excessive rhetoric, stodgy 'techno-scientific' analyses and philosophical and literary attempts at giving it historical and human depth. These three kinds of discourse correspond neatly to the three levels of the institutional construction of the relationship: the political, the economic and the 'civil society'. These three levels in turn determine the three categories of actor: the politicians, the technocrats and those who lead 'civil society'. A few examples give an idea of the general ethos surrounding this project. Let us start with the the politicians.

> The Euro-Mediterranean partnership, inaugurated during the Conference of Barcelona in 1995, defines a policy with objectives that are ambitious and long-term (the Barcelona process). It should be distinguished from earlier European Union policies vis-à-vis the Mediterranean, which gave more importance to development assistance than to a partnership among equals. The greater commitment that followed the declaration of Barcelona originated in the European Union's vital strategic interests in its immediate Mediterranean neighbours [...] The main objectives of the Euro-Mediterranean partnership are: 1) the creation of a zone of peace and stability, based on the principles of human rights and democracy; 2) the construction of a zone of shared prosperity by the gradual setting up of an area of free trade between the European Union and its Mediterranean partners and between these same partners, accompanied by a large financial support from the Community to facilitate economic transition and help partners deal with the socio-economic challenges caused by this transition; 3) the improvement of mutual understanding between the peoples of the region and the promotion of

free and flourishing civil society, thanks to the organization of cultural exchanges, the development of human resources and support for civil societies and social development.[15]

This extract from a report on the Euromed project by one of the top officials on the European side is a model of its kind. There is the wordy core, from which stem, in successive layers, the other elements of the Euro-Mediterranean rhetoric: peace, stability, human rights and democracy, then prosperity and free trade and finally social development, the emergence of civil society and the increase in cultural exchanges between the two sides of the Mediterranean, which should close the virtuous circle of this new kind of partnership.

It is because the relationship is to cover these three fields that it must be based on a partnership because 'the Barcelona Conference', we are told, 'has transformed Mediterranean policy into a global, coherent approach, respectful of a certain balance between the different fields. By combining the three constituents within a global policy, it recognizes that there is no use having a separate approach to financial, economic, cultural and security questions.'[16] But that is not all. It is less the overall approach (the three constitutive elements) than in the ways in which it will be put into operation that gives this partnership its originality. Numerous declarations, regulatory texts and analyses stress that:

> the different partners must meet and discuss together the framework, preferably multilateral, of the projects being proposed. Dialogue is here the key word for this regional innovation. One of the main achievements of the Euro-Mediterranean partnership has been the carrying on of political dialogue in the context of the Barcelona process, even while the peace process in the Near East was at an impasse. The partnership continues to be the only multilateral political framework within which the representatives of Syria and Lebanon participate regularly with their Israeli counterparts.[17]

People do indeed meet and talk a lot about the Euro-Mediterranean framework because this is one of its most ambitious objectives: 'to create a permanent dialogue between twenty-seven partners who are all very different from one another', as explained by the Barcelona conference programme. To do this, a host of 'exchange venues' have been set up to promote consensus in all fields and at all levels of decision-making.

There are the conferences (four in five years), which bring together the diplomatic heads of the twenty-seven states, but also regular meetings of the ministries of foreign affairs, those of the steering committee of the partnership among the ambassadors, that are more frequent (every quarter), those of the ministries in their respective fields (interior, economy and finance, trade, agriculture, etc.), and those of the top government officials, especially in the field of security. They have even gone to far as to set up networks such as the institutes for foreign policy (EuroMesCo), whose headquarters is at Malta, which organize training seminars for Euro-Mediterranean diplomats. As the European promoters like to repeat: 'The most important thing is to establish trust among the partners, which is the basis of dialogue.' Indeed, the institutionalization of dialogue appears as one of the main objectives of the future Euro-Mediterranean charter for peace and stability.

Hence, to consolidate this institutionalization, it was decided to reach beyond decision-makers and technocrats. There is an increasing number of Euro-Mediterranean networks and opportunities for encounters: the 'Civil Forum' is bringing together the parliamentarians on both sides of the sea, as well as university staff, artists and the NGO leaders who are working in the new fields of human rights, the press, humanitarian and social activities, and so on. The important capitals around the Mediterranean – in Italy, Spain and France, but also in Morocco, Tunisia and Egypt – warmly welcome these meetings, conferences and training seminars, which bring together intellectuals, journalists and militants on both sides of the sea, to discuss Euro-Mediterranean issues. The discussions are featured in the press and on radio, television and the Internet, where numerous sites are dedicated to the subject. Newspapers and magazines give importance to this information, while journals and scholarly reviews dedicate whole issues to the phenomenon.

In spite of the differences of style, according to the different fields and type of actors, the general attitude is very favourable to the project. This was the case particularly at the start, in the wake of the Barcelona Conference. But at the end of the first cycle, when its mediocre results became apparent, criticisms began to surface, particularly in Marseilles in 2000, when the first balance sheets were drawn up. Results were well below expectations.

Nevertheless, the Euro-Mediterranean partnership project was presented in the official discourses by politicians and diplomats as the ultimate solution for helping the countries south of the Mediterranean to evolve in a positive manner and it continues to appear, in 'scientific' texts, as the 'best path' for economic and social development, as well as for its interventions in 'civil society'. Diplomatic rhetoric is thus reinforced by a scholarly discourse.

For example, in the journal *Confluences*, which dedicated several numbers to the project, a certain Agnès Chevalier wrote:

> The Euro-Mediterranean agreements are substantially different from previous development assistance agreements. They are based on the principle of adherence to disciplinary rules and a series of values. In the traditional fields of economic aid, particularly commercial preferences, and financial assistance, the approach has been radically changed. Commercial preferences will from now on be reciprocal for there will be a two-way exchange of trade in industrial products, while European grants will be linked to conditionalities. It is an important change. With commercial reciprocity, the Euro-Mediterranean relationship will no longer be one of assistance, it will become the partnership that has been invoked for so many years (to the point that the EU could seem, in the short term, as the main beneficiary of regional free trade). The prospect is much more demanding for the Mediterranean economies which must open up to competition [...] It is now known that it is only by opening up internationally that the developing economies can hope to improve their standard of living ...[18]

There are dozens of texts of this kind which, purporting to be scientific, repeat normative judgements such as 'it is only by opening up internationally that the developing economies can hope to improve their standard of living' or blatantly inaccurate statements such as 'there will be a two-way exchange of trade in industrial products'. Little attention is given to contrary evidence and diplomatic rhetoric is just given an academic gloss. But such reinforcement seems to give it scientific legitimacy, which makes it more credible at the second level, that of the technocrats, who, in their turn, can use it the better to carry out their work in the field. The training seminars and all the networks connecting the technicians from both sides of the sea have been put in place for an effective dissemination of the messages of this pseudo-science. The purpose of the publications of the Euromed institutions in this field is striking, in view of the objectives being pursued: to spread among the circles concerned a ready-made way of thinking that can easily be used.

Partnership, co-development, sustainable development, free trade, opening the economy, levelling up, liberalization ... a lexicon of this new Euro-Mediterranean political economy should be drawn up. It cleverly hides the real stakes of a political economy, which are much more prosaic.

But, as Samir Amin comments:

> All these proposals stem directly from the exclusive logic of globalized neoliberalism (opening up of the economy, creating a friendly environment for foreign investment, deregulation, dismantling protection, etc.) as it is seen by the United States, the WTO, the World Bank and the IMF. But this logic, which emerges clearly in any analysis of the facts, is drowned in a technicist and normative discourse – the opposite to rational argumentation – the final objective of which is not an analysis of the facts, but justification for political action.

Scholarly discourse has also rallied to its side a technostructure that was already quite won over by the neoliberal logic, even if there have been a few controversies and polemics limited to some specialist fields. However, it was not enough: the partnership project, if it is to be sustainable, must go beyond the narrow confines of the 'leading elites'. It must attract broad sections of the middle classes that are organized or on the way to being organized in the new ties created by associations that the local authorities are forced to tolerate.

This, then, is where the 'civil society' comes in. The discourse on 'human rights' and on 'democracy' thus covers the dryer and less attractive discourse on economic liberalization and the laws of the market – or the still more boring and meaningless language of the politicians:

The concept of partnership aims at creating a real zone of

shared prosperity but it should not limit itself to relationships between states if it really wishes to fulfil its objective of co-development […] It is thus necessary to reinforce and put in place the necessary instruments for decentralized cooperation in order to promote exchanges between the development actors in the framework of internal legislation: those responsible for political and civil affairs, the cultural and religious world, universities, researchers, media, associations, trade unions and private and public enterprises […] To do this, action that supports democratic institutions and the reinforcement of the rule of law and civil society will be supported.[19]

Many forums were then launched to mobilize the human rights militants and other non-governmental associations who, for their part, hoped it would help them to escape the overwhelming pressures of those who governed them and reinforce their capacities for local action. Often it resulted in compromise: anti-liberal democrats and opposition leaders used the opportunity to expand and reinforce their activities by giving them greater visibility. Sometimes it was very useful to denounce wrongful imprisonments, electoral frauds and police brutality – or even state crimes that took place here and there and which local authorities were used to committing with impunity. In these cases, as possibilities to protest had previously been non-existent or limited, the Euro-Mediterranean forums provided unexpected opportunities to continue the struggle.

As far as the European project designers were concerned, this was still not enough. Other categories had to be reached, beyond the 'political society', for it was essential to obtain the largest possible support, thus giving more legitimacy to the 'association project' that they wanted to install.

This was to be the role of the Euromed Civil Forum, which was created in Barcelona and was to function as a 'dialogue agora'. University personnel, personalities from the fields of culture and the arts such as film directors, artists, poets, but also NGO activists representing a wide range of social action, were to be invited to meet, dialogue and exchange experiences in order to construct common grounds that transcend the North–South divide and impart a human dimension to the Euro-Mediterranean political and economic project.

A common Mediterranean civilization is put forward as being a melting pot, giving depth to the project. The humanities and social sciences, particularly history and anthropology, are thus called upon to give the idea its historical legitimacy, as well as literary texts, films and drama. The writings of Taha Hussein and Tewfik Al-Hakim are rediscovered to accentuate the 'Mediterranean' identity of Egypt. Spanish Andalusia is highlighted, to stress both its tolerance and the Mediterranean that it had constructed. The notion of cultural diversity is stressed, both to cover up old antagonisms and attenuate current conflicts, but also to de-emphasize very strong identities, for example the 'Arab' character of the countries on the southern rim which risk resuscitating the 'non-politically correct' issue of the unity of the Arab world or the highly inconvenient question of Israeli colonialism.

Thus the *Mare Nostrum* of the poets is added to the human rights and democracy of opposition militants, to the rationality of the economists in the technostructure, to the far-sightedness of the political leaders to bring the virtuous circle of the Euro-Mediterranean discourse to a harmonious conclusion.

In this way the 'Barcelona Consensus' can function without too many shocks: peace, prosperity, liberty and tolerance, which covers, in a perfectly logical sequence, the different dimensions of the project, as well as the various social actors who have to carry it out. The liberalization of the national economies in the new free trade zone can now start.

The Euromed project, a complex institutional construction However, the 'dialogue', which is a condition of the 'partnership', requires places and spaces that are permanent if it is to be carried out over a long period of time. This is partly the reason why the European designers of the project have concentrated on constructing all these institutions through which the partners have to 'dialogue' and which will be the springboard for decisions and actions. The present authors recognize the very many difficulties in deconstructing such a complex and bureaucratic mechanism and admit perplexity in grasping its objectives. True, the Merton theory of changing the ends by the means enables us to understand, at least partially, the internal logic of this veritable institutional bulimia typical of bureaucracy, as the EU technocrats know very well. Each problem has its committee or commission, its bureaucrats and its experts. But in the case of the Euromed project, events have taken a somewhat farcical turn.

All dimensions of social activity – political, economic, civil and cultural – and all hierarchical levels of decision-making, as well as the social actors involved, have created or will create some institution, committee, commission, council, centre or forum. The Internet makes it possible to connect all those involved in order to ensure, apart from occasional meetings, a 'permanent dialogue' among themselves. Let us not forget that the motto of this extraordinary set-up is dialogue, which is an indispensable condition of partnership. Sometimes, in fact, they have even created institutions for specialized training to help 'the partners' speak the same language, which is of course the one that the European designers of the project want to impose in order to inculcate the new ideology more easily. The virtues of simple dialogue are not enough; there is a 'pedagogy' to be learnt through the training institutes, specialized seminars, etc. This has led a critical observer, Sébastian Sadek, to remark sarcastically: 'Europe cannot respond by creating an infinite series of research centres and academics and then project them on the past in a generalized way.'[20]

Let us have a quick look at this institutional construction. At the political level the conferences bring together the foreign affairs ministers of the twenty-seven countries that are partners in Euromed. Since the one in Barcelona, in November 1995, there have been eleven such meetings, some of them official and others, like think tanks, more informal. There are also regional conferences on policies concerning specific sectors (culture, industrial cooperation, information, energy, local water management, the environment, health, etc.).

However, the most frequent meetings are those of the Euro-Mediterranean Committee on the Barcelona Process, which is the central steering group of the partnership as a whole. These quarterly meetings bring ambassadors together and are intended to adopt policies for regional cooperation between the different partners. It should be noted that, within this framework, the representatives of Syria and Lebanon have been able to meet regularly with their Israeli counterparts. This remarkable achievement is often proudly highlighted by European officials, who see it as a proof of the effectiveness of their peace strategy within the whole project. Thus, in an evaluation report on the first cycle of the Barcelona process, the European Commission stressed that:

Barcelona is the only context for ministerial meetings in which Israel, Syria and the Lebanon participate. This is not without its importance during the last three years when the Middle East peace process has been blocked. Since the Barcelona Conference (1995), the foreign affairs ministers of the twenty-seven partner countries have met periodically, in Malta (1997), Palermo (1998 – informal meeting), Stuttgart (1999) and Lisbon (2000 – informal meeting). In addition, twelve ministerial sectoral meetings have been organized during this period.[21]

A little while after this text was published (September 2000), the second *intifada* broke out – which at least had the merit of seriously weakening the self-satisfaction of the commission. Nevertheless, the European strategists continued to invoke the virtues of dialogue. Still today, after 9/11, and while Israel, led by Sharon, is flouting international law with great brutality and ferocity, the European partners of the countries on the southern Mediterranean are incapable of taking action based on the principles underlying the Barcelona discourse and insist on the need for dialogue. On the bilateral level, the association councils create regular contacts between the officials of the countries concerned by these agreements and their European counterparts.

However, apart from the restricted group of the 'decision-makers', it is felt that there is need for greater dialogue and involvement of the technicians and experts responsible for implementing the directions given by the politicians. In this framework, many meetings bring together the senior officials responsible for policy and security coordination on questions as diverse as peace-building, human rights, conflict prevention and the work programme of the Euro-Mediterranean network of foreign policy research institutes.[22]

EuroMesCo is the name of this network, composed of thirty-seven research institutes situated on both sides of the Mediterranean, which are to organize training seminars in five fields: political dialogue and security among the partnership, interdependencies, foreign policy and mutual security (the PESC programme), sub-regional cooperation and governance issues. These are aimed mainly at the young diplomats and administrators who will be working in the different sectors of the partnership. Consulting the website of this network, we have been able to read the texts prepared by the discussion leaders on the theme of political and security dialogue – texts disseminated by the journal created for this purpose. We were astonished to see the analyses dedicated to peace in the Mediterranean dismissing the Israeli–Palestinian conflict as a corny problem of 'intolerance' and 'fundamentalism' and covering up, courtesy of rhetoric about peace between people, the sinister colonial reality of Israeli policy.

A new programme, 'culture for peace and human rights', has just been launched by the European Commission and should receive trainees regularly from the twenty-seven states. One can already imagine what texts the future trainees will have to study and what ideas will be presented to them.

Besides the decision-makers and the experts, the Euromed project should also involve elected politicians. Thus the Parliamentary Euro-Mediterranean Forum has been created. It will bring together parliamentarians of the Mediterranean countries participating in the Barcelona process, the national parliaments of the member states of the European Union, as well as the European Parliament. It meets annually, but has a permanent strucuture which ensures follow-up activities between the sessions. This institution functions as a place for dialogue, but also as a 'transmission belt' that should convey the Euromed activities and projects under way to the political classes in each country.

Decision-makers, experts and elected representatives cannot escape the need for dialogue and its implications in the Barcelona process. The institution becomes a genuine constraint, the strength of which many of the actors on the southern side, who have been used to the individual action of despotism, have not yet understood. As its European project designers have remarked:

> The potential of the Barcelona process cannot be fully realized until the countries in the region have generally 'appropriated' the process. More efforts can be made to explain the objectives and advantages of the process and to turn it into an active and vibrant partnership [...] Greater visibility should be given to all the projects that have received aid from it, so a 'Euro-Mediterranean partnership' label will be given to it.[23]

At the economic and financial level there is the same institutional 'architecture', with its different stages corresponding to the various categories of actors (decision-makers, experts, elected representatives and civil society), as well as all the ways in which questions will be tackled: forums, networks, training institutes, etc.

MEDA is the name of all these economic and financial programmes around which the Euro-Mediterranean project is constructed. It is led by a permanent steering committee and based on the European delegations in the different countries of the southern Mediterranean, which constitute the local support for development actions.

There is no need here to go into a detailed analysis of all the institutions that have been created to organize and implement the projects. But, just as at the political level, the overall logic remains the same, in spite of the complexity and diversity of the sectors concerned, which is far greater here. In other words, the aim is to bring together and involve as many agents as possible so that they 'appropriate' this logic and internalize it.

Banks, business centres, transport, energy, water, agriculture and the environment are thus more or less seen in a framework of action at the national level (the setting up of business centres in Egypt, Jordan, Morocco and Tunisia), as well as at regional level (the Femise network of institutes for economic research), while the more or less regular forums are open to the chambers of commerce or, in the framework of the Unimed network, to the employers' organizations. In such cases the aims of the dialogue are cleverly linked to training sessions: 'emphasis is put on the practical aspects of how to structure and manage an employers' organization or how to analyse the reform of external assistance programmes'. In the framework of industrial cooperation and in order to accelerate 'the economic transition', representatives of the private sector are increasingly invited to participate and play an active role in the implementation of projects.

Here, too, the involvement of 'civil society' is encouraged. In each of the twenty-seven countries, Economic and Social Councils (CES)[24] and similar institutions are encouraged to organize themselves into a permanent forum 'in order to contribute to a better understanding of the important issues concerning the Euro-Mediterranean partnership'. At their meeting in November 2000 the representatives of these councils 'call on the Ministries of Foreign Affairs to recognize the importance of annual social and professional summits, the usefulness of the projects that result from these encounters and the need for a dialogue that is permanent and structured with organized civil society'.[25] This involvement is important because it gives legitimacy to the European action in the economic and social fields. The social effects of the transition towards the market economy and the privatizations of the public sector will, in fact, be tough and hard to swallow – especially for the working classes. By accepting the principle of this transition, the CES give it their sanction and limit their role to managing its effects through using (or, rather, under-using) social protection systems, which will be transformed, and also the migratory pressures, which will be reinforced. As for the latter, which is of primary concern to European countries, an action programme that becomes 'legitimate' through this involvement thus becomes possible:

> Action will concentrate on the following items: activities concerning the right of asylum and the protection of refugees; cooperation in the struggle against illegal immigration and the traffic in human beings in particular; the treatment of migration questions, in particular the social integration of migrants who legally reside in a member state and co-development activities with their country of origin; conformity of the judiciary systems, especially the laws concerning the family and inheritance; cooperation in the fight against organized crime through the training of legal and police officials.[26]

As can be seen, the dynamics of the process include dialogue and pedagogy with, of course, the underlying purpose of making the 'partners' in the South 'share' the postulates and ideas of the European project. For example, 'conformity of the judiciary systems [...] and the laws concerning the family' is accompanied, to be more effective, with the 'training of legal and police officials'.

We have already seen how civil society has been called upon, at the political and economic levels, to participate through parliamentary forums or employers' organizations or the Economic and Social Councils. But it is only considered as a complementary structure to the economic and social reforms that should guide the political leaders and their respective technostructures. We can now deal with the civil society as such, which is seen as a whole and relatively autonomous of the state and the political sphere. The associations or NGOs that compose it cover the same sectors of social life as are administered by public policies – or are supposed to do so – but their activities follow a different logic from that of the opposition parties and public officials. Some of them, for example in the field of human rights and democracy, can oppose the activities of the state, while others, in the humanitarian or ecological fields may supplement, or even replace them outright.[27] But all are – in principle – independent of the state and not much concerned by the strategies of political power, either local or national.

For a long time the political systems of the countries to the south of the Mediterranean, which were organized on the single-party model, had prohibited, or barely tolerated, all forms of association that risked competing with their monopoly over society. Since the 1980s, triumphant neoliberalism has cleverly been accompanied by a liberating, democratic and humanitarian discourse, which made it attractive and enabled it to be imposed on the middle classes, who had grown tired of the straitjacket of despotism. At the same time, the leading elites of these countries, who were unable to resist the Structural Adjustment Programmes and neoliberal reforms imposed by the international institutions (IMF, World Bank and the WTO) and the Western countries, were forced to adjust their power system to the new norms and thus to accept the principle of independent associations. This is the particular historical background which explains the rapid emergence of civil society in this region and the new political issues that this introduces into politics.

This political and strategic dimension has obviously not escaped the attention of the European promoters of the Euro-Mediterranean partnership project and they consider it as a key to their action. It is through the civil society that the 'Barcelona consensus' can become effective, by outflanking, in the Hegelian sense of the word *aufgehoben*, the limits of political power that its authoritarian exercise has reduced to cliques linked to society only through clientelism. It is also through civil society that it is possible to get round possible resistance by the state and the remains of populism and nationalism that it harbours. And it is thanks to civil society that the painful realities of neoliberal reform and the shameful compromises on peace can be more easily swallowed or 'appropriated' as the EU documents put it. Cunningly wrapped up in an insipid mantle of humanitarianism, human rights and democracy, the hard core of the future association will be more easily accepted by the social groups that do not expect much from their state and who pragmatically take over the spaces left free as it is weakened.

This is not the place for an exhaustive listing of the many NGOs created in the framework of the Euromed project. Concerned as they are with the economic and social sectors, but also the cultural and artistic, they have profited from the benevolence of the MEDA programme, which has financed dozens of them. It is to bring them together that the Barcelona Conference created the Euromed Civil Forum, which has been given a permanent follow-up committee. Dozens of projects lead to the regular creation of NGOs, networks, observatories and other institutions that concern the sectors covered by national policies, but which are dealt with outside official state circuits. For, as a senior official of the European Commission has emphasized, 'we support the citizen and civil society. The governments can go very far by working with each other, but it is never enough.'[28]

The importance given by European strategy to the involvement of civil society in the countries of the southern rim of the Mediterranean is not just window-dressing. As we have already seen, it is playing a major role in the European determination to establish political and economic commitments through inter-state agreements, but also to involve the whole society through its association network. In fact, in their evaluation of the first five years of the Barcelona process, the rapporteurs link this question to the success of the whole process:

> A free and prosperous civil society is a basic precondition
> for the success of the partnership in all its aspects. The non-
> governmental organizations acting in a legal framework
> can make a most useful contribution in various fields of the
> partnership [...] Constructive action, particularly the sup-
> port given to NGOs, must be financed as part of the national
> MEDA programmes, as well as the MEDA programme to
> promote democracy. Financial aid given by MEDA must be
> more subordinated to real progress in these fields.[29]

Through this scarcely disguised threat of the European Commissioner can be seen the importance that 'civil society' plays in the arrangements being made by the EU to involve the countries of the southern rim of the Mediterranean in neoliberal reform. We should remember that, when the first Structural Adjustment Programmes were launched in Africa, the strategies of the IMF and the World Bank, which were picked up by the large American foundations like Ford and Rockefeller, as well as other US and Canadian programmes, redirected parts of their funding to African countries, particularly towards the intellectuals, university personnel and other activist groups from the middle classes. There, too, democracy and human rights were heavily emphasized and the mobilizing strength of the discourse had worked, almost for the same reasons as in the present case. The powers of the state had become veritable fortresses that the classic forms of political opposition could not shake and external support for strong and independent civil societies was warmly welcomed. But while the African militants and intellectuals were thinking in terms of the 'democratic transition', the strategists of the Washington consensus were aiming at weakening the state in order to put their notorious SAPs into operation. Since then the economies have been to a large extent broken up, privatized and opened to the world market, but in many countries the democratization of the governing institutions remains yet to be implemented.

It goes without saying that the authors of this text in no way wish to act as the bird of evil omen for the southern Mediterranean countries. However, the European commitment to support strong civil societies in their countries and to encourage democracy and human rights must be carefully analysed. It is true that this has facilitated and can continue to facilitate the development of a social and political dynamic that can impose a relative opening up of local dictatorships. However, linked as it is to the neoliberal strategy of the project as a whole, which has nothing whatsoever of democracy about it, it is serving as an instrument, rather than as an end in itself. On the other hand the heavy, verbose insistence in the Euro-Mediterranean discourse on this aspect of the process can also be seen as a ruse to persuade part of the population of these countries (the middle classes) to support the Barcelona process by playing on their own demands (more liberties, democratization, etc.), while minimizing or even shrugging off its dramatic economic and social consequences (greater unemployment, pauperization, etc.).

Like its predecessor in Washington, the Barcelona consensus is also a complex ideological construct elaborated to assist the neoliberal project. It is based on dialogue and the persuasion of the 'elites', gaining access to the middle classes of the southern Mediterranean countries, and it is trying to get them so deeply involved in the whole process that it becomes irreversible. The consensus wants 'partners' – as long as the consensus itself can construct them. But like all discourses of this kind, it ends by inverting the order of means and ends, causes and consequences, 'the virtual and the real'.[30] By ignoring the hard facts that the proposed action will have to face, sooner or later, it conjures up, like Dr Pangloss in Voltaire's *Candide*, 'the best of all possible worlds'.

The Euro-Mediterranean project: beyond the discourse
Europe, Euromed and its 'partners' south of the Mediterranean
Europe and the policies of the European Union were at the origin of the Euromed project. It was Europe that conceived, constructed and implemented it. Throughout our investigation, we were struck by the fact that in all the official texts, solemn declarations, technical and political evaluations, as well as in meetings with cadres and 'NGOs', it is the European Union that is the 'master of ceremonies', vis-à-vis the countries south of the Mediterranean, who remain passive and cautious. The structure of the whole Barcelona process has been worked out by the Europeans, in the form of legislative and regulatory texts, with the role of the southern Mediterranean countries being reduced to ratifying them.

The working group meetings, like the large conferences and the forums, are almost all held in large European cities, the economic metropole and real nerve centre of the process being Brussels, while the symbolic capital is Barcelona. In the southern Mediterranean countries, the European Union has set up 'national delegations' which depend on their European headquarters and work with those giving the orders, who are located in Europe.[31] It is the European Union that establishes, through its senior officials and experts, the priorities for action and funding methods, with the countries south of the Mediterranean being brought in later on to organize implementation in the field.

The partners It is the European Union that chooses which countries come within the Euromed framework. On the one side, there are all the European countries integrated into the EU and which thus constitute a collective unity with a common organization and a shared strategy. On the other side, there are the southern Mediterranean states, with no unifying force except their common geographical situation in this region.[32] Most of them are Arab, but they have been arbitrarily separated from the other countries of the Arab world with whom, however, they form a relatively homogeneous entity. They already have an international representation, the Arab League, even if it is somewhat latent, ineffective and powerless. The recognized powerlessness of this institution, like the Union of the Arab Maghreb (UAM), reflects the decline of the states in this region and their inability to give organic form (economic and political) to what is an evident historical and cultural unity. Playing on this weakness, the EU, after having 'baptized' these Arab countries as 'Mediterranean', insists on associating them with the State of Israel (because it is situated on the southern Mediterranean?), which not only has nothing in common (economic, technological, etc.) with the other countries, but which is occupying Palestine by force, is at war with Syria and Lebanon and is in conflict, to a greater or lesser degree, with the others. It follows, using this 'Carolingian' logic, that Finland, which stretches almost to the North Pole, is involved in Euromed, because it belongs to the EU, while Mauritania, which is Arab and forms part of the UAM, and Libya, remain outside the process: the first because it is 'oceanic' and the second because it is 'under embargo'.[33]

The European architects of the process have decided: the countries of the southern Mediterranean are included because of their geographical situation or their 'docility', while the inclusion of the European states depends on their economic and political integration. Thus the criteria for inclusion are not the same. Nevertheless, in spite of its apparent arbitrariness, there is a reason for this difference in treatment for it facilitates the integration of Israel into the Arab world with the hope, eventually, of seeing this country 'accepted' by its neighbours. The aim is to bypass, using economic logic, the conflicts between Israel and the Arab countries. This is the strategic dimension of the consensus of Barcelona, in which both the naïveté and the timorous, hypocritical nature of the European approach to the conflict are all too apparent.

On the other hand, the flagrant denial of the Arab character of most of the southern partners[34] in favour of the tenuously relevant, but more consensual 'Mediterranean' epithet enables the EU to dodge the complexity of its relationships with the Arab world, as well as avoiding any embarrassment for the American leadership. For the United States, the Israeli–Palestinian conflict, like their hegemony over the oil countries of the Arabian Gulf, is their own preserve, which must be strictly respected by the European Union.[35] This was quite brazenly pointed out by Christopher Patten, the European Commissioner in charge of Mediterranean affairs: 'The negotiations are primarily the responsibility of the parties involved. But there is a role for the international community to support the process, and the European Union for its part attaches great importance to that task [...] But we need to work in close cooperation with the United States [...] Europe cannot and should not compete with that work, or cut across it.'

Thus, as we can see, the architecture of the partnership imposed by the European Union on the Arab and Mediterranean countries must be fitted into the existing hierarchy of positions at the world level. The strategic interests of the EU come 'after' those of the United States. Euromed expresses both the economic power of the European Union over its southern neighbours and its strategic weakness vis-à-vis the United States. The consensus of Barcelona is also to be interpreted in this triangular relationship, even though the third partner, the United States, does not figure much in its discourse.

It should also be noted that the relationships of 'partnership' presented by the Barcelona discourse as the great innovation of this kind of association are basically unequal or asymmetrical. In fact, each of the southern Mediterranean states separately negotiates an association agreement, together with its implementation, with the European Union. The 'multilateralism' is therefore one-way: a powerful collection of states, with a common international strategy vis-à-vis weak national bodies that are not united in the process – indeed sometimes even rivals with one another in certain sectors such as agriculture or tourism. It is the logic of the 'group' as opposed to that of the 'series'[36] and the inevitable domination of the former over the latter.[37] This domination becomes evident in the official documents in spite of all efforts to camouflage it. It is the European Commission that fixes the objectives, in the form of injunctions and duties that the southern partners must follow: 'The ad hoc meetings of senior officials, such as are currently being held, must be transformed into an institutional forum of dialogue on questions of policy and security and mechanisms must be created to promote effective joint action in the fields of terrorism, conflict prevention and crisis management.'[38]

There are times when the Commission itself issues a veritable call to order:

> The Commission calls on Egypt to sign the association agreement and invites Lebanon, Syria and Algeria to collaborate with the Union to accelerate the negotiations so that they can be completed between now and June 2001, at latest [...] The Commission calls on the Member States to take the necessary measures to accelerate the ratification of the agreement with Jordan and guarantee that the subsequent agreements are ratified during the two years following signature.[39]

And it is always the Commission that determines the agendas and the deadlines:

> For each country that has signed an association agreement, it is necessary to examine in detail the measures to be taken to carry out a greater, reciprocal liberalization of trade in the field of agriculture, from now on to the end of the transition period, according to the applicable arrangements of GATT and the WTO [...] All countries signing an association agreement with the EU must, during the course of the following five years at latest, complete free trade agreements with all the other signatories of association agreements.[40]

What is clear is that the Arab states are required to accept the principle of the integration of Israel in a single market. Here we find the initial trick: the constitution of twenty-seven partners in this roundabout way, imposing the admission of Israel without it having to fulfil all the political preconditions. And finally, the European officials lose no opportunity to recall that it is the EU that finances the programmes and it threatens to make the funds allocated conditional on the behaviour of the countries: ' ... the relationship between the application of the association agreements and funding in the MEDA framework must be clarified, and future financial aid should be subordinated to the desire of partners to pursue the objectives of the agreements as concerns the economic transition'.[41]

These few examples – among many others – show that the discourse about partnership functions as an ideology in the strict sense of the term, that is, as 'an inverted image of the real'. The reality is that there is an inequality in power between the north and south Mediterranean, the European supervisors confronting states that are their clients. Euromed is just a new, non-colonial form of domination based on the structural inequality of its European and Mediterranean components. Through the smokescreen of the Barcelona discourse, the dominated countries of the south have become 'partners' and the neoliberal reform process that is imposed upon them becomes an 'association'.

The state of the art There have been many studies on the asymmetric and unequal character of the position of the EU countries and that of their Mediterranean partners. Here we shall just give the salient points: for more details readers are referred to the statistical data at the end of this book.

The inequality in the levels of national production is far greater than in other analogous situations, for example, the USA and Mexico in NAFTA. The GNP of Belgium alone, considered a small country within the European Union, is estimated at 230 billion dollars – more than that of nine Arab Mediterranean countries. In general the per capita income gap ranges from 1 to 10, taking Egypt in comparison with Denmark. These gaps in revenue must not only be seen in economic, but also in social and cultural terms. The rate of unemployment in the active population reaches 30 per cent in the southern countries and in certain situations (Morocco, Algeria) close to 40 per cent, with very strong pressures on the lowering of wages which, in turn, affect large parts of the informal – or unregulated – economy and/or migration towards Europe. This reservoir of labour is utilized by states to deregulate the labour market and dismantle the social security systems that had been set up on the welfare state model in the aftermath of independence during the 1960s. The labour reservoir thus promotes the 'economic reforms' that the southern Mediterranean countries have started and that the Barcelona process is trying to complete.

Meanwhile, the public authorities and business are cleverly manipulating rivalry between workers in order to weaken the trades unions. Associations of the unemployed[42] have been created almost everywhere, while there are fewer and fewer possibilities of legal redress (through workers' councils or work inspection) against increasing abuses of authority. But globalization, with its ideological effects and its new methods of 'social work', is already prepared to intervene: the 'war against poverty' replaces the 'class struggle', which is no longer politically correct, while humanitarian volunteers are gradually taking the place of the old militant trades unionists. As we shall see later, religious associations are rushing into the breach thus opened, finding no difficulty in recruiting among the popular classes that have been abandoned by the state. The Islamic opposition has become a popular force.

The Human Development Index (HDI)[43] puts the EU countries in fifteenth place, while the countries south of the Mediterranean are positioned in eightieth place and this would be even lower if Israel (twenty-third place) were not counted among them. According to this index, the literacy rates of adults in the southern Mediterranean countries are still about 50 per cent (15 per cent for women), while illiteracy has been virtually eliminated in the EU countries. It is true that the numbers of children and adolescents at school have grown enormously since the independence of these countries and the average attendance is now from 60 to 70 per cent, but unfortunately, as the latest estimates[44] indicate, these statistics are not going to rise. Rather, they will fall as a result of the large reduction in public expenditure, which is considered unproductive by the World Bank strategists and implemented by the Structural Adjustment Programmes.

Up until now the southern Mediterranean Arab countries have allocated a small proportion of their national revenue to education (an average of 4 per cent) and scientific research (an average of 0.3 per cent), which places these countries well behind the European Union and even after Latin American and Asian countries with a similar economic level. Even so, these thresholds, modest as they are, were linked to welfare state public policies and it is likely that the abandoning of these methods of state regulation, which began with the Structural Adjustment Programmes, will continue during the Barcelona process. The gaps between the southern Mediterranean countries and those of the European Union will thus widen and adversely affect the whole problem of growth in the former countries. The new strategies being developed in these fields are evident:

increasing privatization in education, which is strongly supported by the devotees of the new economy, and the switch of research from the public centres to private enterprise, with the gradual abandoning of pure science in favour of applied science. All this is taking place against a background of 'brain drain' towards the Western countries that the new European policies of 'selection immigration' are now preparing to supervise.

However, it is above all in the process of insertion of the southern Mediterranean countries into the world economy where they are most vulnerable. This is evident from the following statistics. In 1998, intra-regional trade between them was estimated at about $9.5 billion (i.e. 3 per cent of the total), but $4.5 billion if Israel and Turkey are excluded, compared with $113 billion for trade with the European Union (if Israel and Turkey are excluded). For comparison, the intra-regional trade of Asian countries belonging to ASEAN and the Latin American countries of MERCOSUR is nearly 25 per cent, which leaves the southern Mediterranean countries trailing well behind both these regions. This is all the more serious in that almost 50 per cent of the trade of these countries is carried out with the European Union alone.

This exceptional 'verticality' of trade with the European Union puts the countries of the southern Mediterranean in an extremely dependent situation vis-à-vis the EU, as well as promoting vigorous rivalry between them concerning the goods and services that they sell on the European market. It makes horizontal cooperation between them more difficult – not to mention South–South regional integration policies. This is exactly what the EU strategists want. They have seized the opportunity of complimenting Tunisia, citing it as an example of good integration. In their 1999 report,[45] they emphasized: 'Trade relations with Tunisia are very good and show that this country is well integrated into the European market (78 per cent of exports and 72 per cent of imports from Tunisia are with the EU). Consequently, Tunisia has already anticipated, since 1996, the dismantling of its tariffs with a view to a gradual establishment of bilateral free trade zones with the other Mediterranean countries, i.e. Morocco and Egypt.' The dependency becomes more apparent when the economic structure and the trade of the two regions are analysed. The southern Mediterranean countries import manufactured products that are high value-added (machinery and equipment goods, medicines, high-tech services) and export mainly agricultural products and textiles. This is responsible for the structural trade deficits with the EU – deficits that are constantly growing. In 1990 the EU imported an approximate value of 28 billion euros from the southern Mediterranean countries and exported 37 billion euros; in 2000, it imported 63 billion euros, but exported 85 billion euros.

Other sources of external revenue for the southern Mediterranean countries are the émigré labour in Europe, tourism (Egypt, Tunisia, Morocco) and hydrocarbons (Algeria). In most cases, the external trade balance of these countries thus depends on two or three products, the price fluctuations of which depend mainly on the European market which gives no commercial preferences to its Mediterranean partners. Thus it is that the Common Agricultural Policy that the European countries have maintained after the WTO meeting at Doha in November 2001 continues to tax the products of these countries heavily, while insisting that they open their customs barriers as required by the Barcelona process. In comparison with Mexico, the 'rate of opening' (relationship of exports to imports) for the southern Mediterranean countries is much greater: 39 per cent for Morocco, 42 per cent for Algeria, 82 per cent for Tunisia, while for Mexico it is 22 per cent. Over the last few decades, the countries of the southern Mediterranean have been forced to accept the increase in their trade deficit in food products while the stereotype still prevailing in the West classes them as agricultural countries. Today Egypt, Morocco and Tunisia have to import more than a third of their cereal consumption, while Algeria imports two-thirds. Tunisia and Morocco, exporters of vegetables until the 1970s, are now importing them, as well as edible oils, the imports of which have increased 200 per cent in a decade. We agree with Susan George that it is in this context that we should view the debts of the southern Mediterranean countries, the levels of which put them above the average of other developing countries.

The World Bank classes Algeria and Jordan among the 'severely indebted' middle-income countries; Morocco, Tunisia and Turkey are 'moderately indebted' while Egypt is a MILIC (Moderately Indebted Low-Income Country). According to these figures, we see nothing very 'moderate' in the levels of indebtedness, just as we cannot note a great difference between these countries that have been classed in different categories.

TABLE 3.1 Debt burden in $ per head of the population and as a percentage of the Gross National Product

Country	$$ per head of population[46]	Interest as % of GNP in 1994	Stock debt as % of GNP in 1994
Algeria	1,119	4.5	74.3
Egypt	553	3.2	78.9
Jordan	1,439	3.5	121.8
Morocco	869	3.8	76.3
Tunisia	1,076	3.4	60.8
Turkey	1,113	3.1	51.4
Average	1,028	3.6	77.25
GRP MIMIC*	892	2.2	46.1
GRP SIMIC**	1,384	1.6	37.7
All developing countries	480	1.8	37.7

Notes: * MIMIC = Moderately Indebted Middle-Income Country   ** SIMIC = Severely Indebted Middle-Income Country

Table 3.1 shows that the southern Mediterranean countries have a much greater debt, whatever the yardstick chosen, than the average developing country. The debt stocks of these countries, in relation to their GNP, are far greater than those of developing countries. And all of them, observes Susan George, pay interest, in relation to their GNP, that is far higher than those of other groups: twice that for the developing countries as a whole, more than double the average for the 'severely indebted', two-thirds more than those that are 'moderately indebted'. The infernal logic of international indebtedness is such that countries that docilely accept to settle the contractual servicing of their debt, like Tunisia and Morocco – often cited by the IMF as 'good examples of what should be done, economically and financially' – not only find themselves at the same point as they were fifteen years ago, but they also lag behind in the social field.[47] As Bichara Khader[48] has astutely pointed out: 'Apart from these figures, what is more alarming is that debt feeds corruption, promotes "capital flight" and gives rise to a "new social class" whose economic strength depends on capital linked to international development and the export revenue from primary products. Overall, the "aid" and indebtedness system has contaminated the political field which, nourished from outside, can thus survive without a social base.' The EU is the main creditor of the countries south of the Mediterranean, holding 50 per cent of the debt. There is thus nothing in the 'Barcelona process' that commits the European countries in this field.

Economic dependence and international indebtedness exacerbate even further the effects that the strong demographic pressure exercises on the labour market. It is true that the countries of the southern side of the Mediterranean have started their 'demographic transition', but its effects will not really be felt for at least another two decades. During the last forty years, their populations have multiplied by 2.5, with demographic growth rates averaging 3 per cent. This average has now dropped to less than 2.2 per cent. But, for the time being, these countries have a considerable 'demographic surplus' – over 35 per cent of the population under fifteen years and only a little less than 4 per cent of the population over sixty years. During the 'Thirty Glorious Years', Europe drew on this labour reservoir to complete its reconstruction and relaunch its growth. This labour also helped to rejuvenate the European populations, which were rapidly growing older, for from being temporary, migration became permanent through 'family regrouping'. In this win-win situation, the European countries benefited from cheap and relatively docile labour, while the countries south of the Mediterranean also benefited from having a labour market less under pressure and relatively large external resources from emigrant earnings. This was particularly true of Morocco, Tunisia and Egypt (which 'exported' its labour to the Gulf countries). Tables 3.2 and 3.3 show the extent of these migratory cycles.[49]

At the end of the Thirty Glorious Years and with its economic crisis, Europe decided to slow down the migratory movement and today they talk of stopping it altogether or, rather, creating 'selective' policies.[50] It is the opposite situation in the countries south of the Mediterranean, as they are more than ever before confronted by strong pressures from the younger population (born during the times of independence) who are demanding training, work and income, which the states are incapable of supplying. It is calculated that the three Maghreb countries will see the arrival on the labour market of 2.6 million active people over the next ten years. But the European 'partners', for various reasons – not at all in the 'spirit of Barcelona'

TABLE 3.2 Percentage of foreigners in some European countries[51]

Country	Foreigners as a % of total population (1983)	Foreigners as a % of total population (1993)	Active foreigners as a % of total population (1993)
France	6.8	6.3*	6.2
Germany	7.4	8.5	8.8
Italy	0.7	1.7	?
Belgium	9.0	9.1	8.3
Netherlands	3.8	5.1	3.9

– do not seem ready to respond to the request of the southern Mediterranean countries and even make them compete with the countries of central and eastern Europe. All the while, the migratory pressure, which is becoming stronger and stronger, has been taken over by informal and illegal circuits. Clandestine immigration has become one of the strategic elements of Euro-Mediterranean relationships and a key issue in the Barcelona process, although it is now treated under the heading of security.

To conclude this rapid survey, it might be imagined that the Barcelona process and the 'consensus' on which it is built constitute a commitment to give the southern partners priority treatment. Many who believed this are now disenchanted. They are victims of the illusions created by the 'consensus' and sometimes of their own wishful thinking. Now, not only do they have to face the harsh

TABLE 3.3 Percentage of foreign population from southern Mediterranean[52]

Country	Total foreign population (1993)	Algeria	Morocco	Tunisia	Turkey
Belgium	920.6	1.1	15.8	0.7	9.6
France	3,596.6	17.1	15.9	5.7	5.5
Germany	6,878.1	0.2	1.2	0.4	27
Italy	987.4	0.5	9.9	4.5	–
Netherlands	779.8	–	21.1	0.3	26
Spain	430.4	–	14.2	–	–

realities that this 'process' is producing, but also to deal with those that the 'process' has refused to acknowledge.

The Barcelona process The Barcelona process should be seen against a background of the changing relationships of the countries south of the Mediterranean with Europe since the independence of the former in the 1950s (and in 1962 for Algeria). Subsequently, there has been the gradual construction of the European Union and continuing transfer of the national sovereignty of European states to the European Commission in Brussels, as well as the affirmation of the EU as a central economic pole of the Triad, together with the United States and Japan, in the current globalization movement.

During a first phase, it was the bilateral relationship of the southern Mediterranean countries, particularly those in the Maghreb with France, that was the most important and it was only gradually that the 'multilateral' became the rule, although it was not exclusive. From the 1980s onwards, the public policies of the southern Mediterranean countries that had followed the 'Keynesian' or 'socialist' model ran out of steam and the first Structural Adjustment Programmes, with Morocco and Tunisia, were put into operation. But it was above all in 1992, just after the Gulf War, that the European Union, with its Renewed Mediterranean Policy, declared 'its wish to develop its relationships with the Maghreb in a community framework and to integrate them into a broader space, the Mediterranean'.

The economic orientation is evident: the EU wanted, through increased liberalization, to harmonize its trade in the framework of a globalized economy and the new trends towards regionalization. A few years later in 1995, just after the Oslo agreements, the EU organized a Euro-Mediterranean conference in Barcelona, which started the Barcelona process. Under three headings – political and security; economic and financial; and social and cultural – as well as measures taken to create the 'partnership', the relationships of the European Union with the countries south of the Mediterranean fell squarely within the EU project to create a free trade zone. This was to be unfeignedly in the spirit of the liberalism that has been in fashion since the 1980s, and in close cooperation with the Bretton Woods institutions. Article 2 of the EU Council regulation, which concerns the organization of MEDA (accompanying financial and technical measures), emphasizes this most strongly: 'The country concerned must undertake a reform programme in agreement with the Bretton Woods institutions, or implement programmes that are recognized as being similar, in concertation with these institutions, but not necessarily financially supported by them, in function of the scope and effectiveness of the reforms at the macro-economic level.' It is indeed the MEDA programme which has the responsibility to implement the economic and financial strategy.

Five years have passed and it is possible to draw up a first balance sheet of the process. Here, too, many of the 'well-intentioned' are unsatisfied and consider this balance sheet as disappointing, with some even speaking of failure. As A. Dahmani has observed: 'The fourth Euro-Mediterranean ministerial conference (15–16 November 2000) almost never took place. There were two main reasons: the deterioration of the situation in Palestine and the unsatisfactory results of the Euro-Mediterranean "partnership", recognized by the European Commission itself.'[53]

Nevertheless, as regards the long-term objectives being pursued by the Union, the acceleration of structural adjustment reforms and various contributions to economic transition, the results are not negligible. It is true that only 26 per cent[54] of the credits allocated by the MEDA programme have been used, but the last states, which had hitherto been recalcitrant like Algeria and Syria, ended by signing the association agreements. All in all, of the credits that have been used, almost 70 per cent are linked to Structural Adjustment Programmes or contribute towards the economic transition. (For more details about Tunisia, Morocco and Egypt, consult the Appendix at the end of this book.) For example, as far as Egypt is concerned, the EU evaluation report notes with satisfaction:

> The support given to the industrial modernization programme of Egypt has received the largest amount committed by the EU to any individual project in the framework of the Mediterranean partnership. The PMI (small and medium-sized industries), conceived within the government's programme of economic liberalization, aim at promoting growth and industrial competitiveness in the private sector and at creating a sufficiently sound economic base to enable Egypt to play a major role in the Mediterranean free trade

zone, which is planned for 2010. [...] The PMI aims at helping Egypt to achieve its economic transition from a planned economy to a market economy.[55]

The same self-satisfaction is shown in connection with Tunisia:

> Tunisia is engaged in an ambitious programme of economic reforms. The first structural adjustment facility (FAS I) of 100 million euros was achieved with the disbursement of the second instalment of 60 million euros in 1998. The new programme (FAS II) of 80 million euros was elaborated together with the World Bank and received favourably by the Med Committee in December 1998. The emphasis of the programme has been on continuing privatization and the disengagement of the state, the cleaning up of the financial sector and the reform of secondary and higher education.[56]

For Tunisia, the MEDA has pledged to support the sectoral Structural Adjustment Programme in the field of health and more specifically, health insurance, for which the World Bank had already released a loan of $50 million.

In all the southern Mediterranean countries the Barcelona process is accelerating the privatization programmes by means of financial support to small and medium-sized industries and enterprises, and giving them technical training. The Euromed 'decision-makers' are satisfied, despite an increasing number of warnings. Already in 1998, the Centre Marocain de Conjoncture (CMC) remarked:

> The effects of the free trade zone on our industrial structure and the calculation of its net advantages for the Moroccan economy vary according to sector, the degree of opening and their level of competitiveness. The agreement affects more than 50 per cent of Moroccan imports, in particular shoes, clothes and textiles, food products and drinks [...] The removal of protection will prevent or at least render more difficult the creation of enterprises that are unable to overcome the barriers to entry. There is not only fear of industries disappearing but also of the impossibility of creating new ones. [...] But it should be recalled that the financial support of the EU is above all aimed at ensuring a Moroccan market for

products made in Europe and to enable the Moroccan market to continue reimbursing the interest on its external debt.

The comments of the CMC analysts are shared by most of the observers whose perspicacity has not been impaired by the 'Barcelona consensus'. We know very well, as Bichara Khader has pointed out, 'that the macro-economic effects will not all be positive – quite the contrary […] For Morocco, it is estimated that in twelve years there will have been a loss of almost 3 per cent of the GDP with the collapse of customs revenue […] while 30 to 40 per cent of the Moroccan enterprises could disappear.'[57]

As for Tunisia, the loss of fiscal revenue could amount to 6 per cent of the GDP and there, too, small enterprises unable to survive international competition will disappear. It is indeed these little artisanal and family-based businesses that will be most severely affected by the free trade zone. It is a fact that firms with fewer than ten employees constitute 95 per cent of the enterprises in Egypt, 93 per cent in Jordan, 88 per cent in Lebanon[58] and it is they that create most of the jobs. As we have noted with NAFTA, the customs policy changes in Mexico and the lowering of internal prices have destroyed the artisanal social organization, particularly of the peasants, which has led to a huge migration towards the great cities and particularly to the US frontier where the *maquiladoras* are concentrated.

For Morocco, MEDA plans financing a project – a highway on the northern coast – for 80 million euros, with the idea of attracting the under-employed so they will be less tempted to emigrate to Europe. This region, incidentally, is where most of the kif is grown, a drug sold on the European market. All the Arab countries south of the Mediterranean are confronted by the same conundrum: reform means privatization, but the opening of their frontiers will eventually bring about the disappearance of thousands of small private businesses, in spite of their 'multi-functional' character – so dear to the European defenders of the Common Agricultural Policy.

So we come to foreign investment, for which the Barcelona process envisages very complex incentives, particularly interest bonuses and many guarantees. There is even talk of a Euro-Mediterranean agreement on investment, similar to that of the Multilateral Agreement on Investment (MAI), giving investors guarantees on the security of their activities in case of changes in legislation. MEDA and the European Investment Bank are responsible for this issue.

Unfortunately, however, this famous DFI (direct foreign investment) is not materializing – even from the European countries themselves. This investment is, indeed, eight times less than the US investment in Mexico and fifteen times less than the Japanese investment in south-east Asia! It has been calculated that for Mexico, which received $71 billion in DFI between 1994 and 1999, half of the three million jobs created since then are due to DFI, of which 60 per cent comes from the United States. This compares with the investment from France and Germany – considered the economic pillars of Euromed – in the main Arab countries south of the Mediterranean, which accounted, in 1999, for no more than 1 per cent of all their foreign commitments. In 1999, the twelve southern Mediterranean countries attracted only 2 per cent of the foreign investments of the fifteen countries of the European Union. Paradoxically, their derisory share – around 4 per cent – in the gross capital formation of the countries concerned continues to drop, in spite of the Barcelona process. In 1993 their share had stood at 7 per cent.

Other studies[59] have also emphasized the 'polarizing' effects of these investments: Israel alone benefited from 50 per cent of the European capital invested in the region, followed by Turkey. The rest is shared between Morocco, Tunisia and Egypt. And it is concentrated on the most profit-making sectors, such as offshore industrial activities: textiles and leather goods, mechanical and electrical industries and the energy sector, which attracts the largest proportion of capital (around 80 per cent). In most of these cases, 'these investments do not represent an increase in productive capacity, at a process of capital accumulation as had been the case in the earlier period. The specialization in the national territories is increasingly the result of the decision of the multinationals in placing their activities.'[60]

But was this not the completely logical consequence of the reforms that had been implemented? Is there not a certain naïveté in expecting, as the consensus of Barcelona had made some believe, that 'private investment could take over from the state in the process of developing the country, a job that should also be included in the strategy of industrial and financial multinational groups, whose role is being reinforced by globalization'?[61]

But evidence shows that privatization, because it is motivated by profit, cannot compensate for the regulation that is concerned with broader objectives, such as the 'general interest' of the community, nation, region, province, etc. Latin America has clearly shown over a long period the disastrous results that follow from such substitution. Mexican privatization, for example, has been carried out hastily, and in 1993 there were only 221 enterprises left out of the 1,155 listed in 1983. In the meantime, the national debt had reached $147 billion, the economic and social situation of a large part of the population remained precarious and the country had become heavily dependent on the United States.[62] In Asian countries, particularly China, in contrast, all observers have noted the central role of the state in conducting privatization. Here, the creation of private enterprises, undertaken mostly through the savings of the diaspora, has not come about through a 'dismantling of the public sector', but in addition to it.

It is true that in the Arab states today, their excesses and their failures to carry out their own development policies have created a profound 'disenchantment' among public opinion and this has led to new illusions and expectations placed, this time, on 'privatization'. The Barcelona consensus has cleverly played on this feeling of rejection of 'statism', particularly among the elites, to construct its discourse and legitimize its action. But above all, as can be seen elsewhere, privatization has usually consisted of selling off public assets, as in Egypt, Tunisia, Morocco and Algeria. Privatization thus appears less as a policy that creates new enterprises that enrich the economy – especially industrial – of a country, than a 'sharing out' – by whom and how? – of public property. All this, obviously, is encouraged and financially supported by the Barcelona process.

Thousands of small family and artisan private businesses threatened with closure, direct foreign investment that is not materializing, a national private sector which is developing by 'cannibalizing' the old public sector: these are the main characteristics of the first phase of the Barcelona process and the few corrections included in the second phase have not substantially changed the situation. The privatization movement of the public sector is continuing and now affects all sectors of activity – trade and finance, of course, but also education, health, and soon the basic infrastructures that the commodification logic requires bringing up to standard.[63] The overcrowded 'public' schools are being overtaken by private institutions in which the new middle classes are beginning to invest.

The process starts at the top, with the management institutes and skill centres, and it will eventually cover secondary and primary schools. In Egypt there are now six national private universities and everywhere the public educational system is collapsing under demographic pressure and reduced budgets. There is even a drop in school attendance and also in the quality of training, followed by the reduction in teachers' salaries. Public policy in this sector, remodelled by the new culture, has gradually abandoned the aims of the social state: the 'democratization' of education, which is costly, is not considered useful. What is necessary is a more effective, elitist training. The discourse corresponds to the gaps that are widening between a minority of haves and the great majority of the popular classes for whom there is no question of making any unproductive outlays that will increase the budget deficit. Besides, part of the grassroots training can be carried out by NGOs, for whom the international funding agencies, led by the World Bank, have envisaged a slot in their 'war against poverty' programmes.

Euromed has allocated part of its funds to the 'maintenance of social cohesion', but this also provides an unexpected opportunity for the religious associations to launch into these activities. The gradual disengagement of the state in this sector had started well before the Barcelona process, notably in Morocco, Lebanon and Jordan. In Egypt, it was part of the whole *infitah* policy initiated by President Sadat. In Algeria, it started later, in the 1980s, and the policy is still more cautious than elsewhere, as social resistance is stronger. But increasingly everywhere, access to a good, continuing education is being restricted: it takes up a larger proportion of the family budget than those with low incomes can afford.

This 'two-tier' schooling that the World Bank strategists have made general throughout the southern countries of the Mediterranean combines with a two-tier health system, like the one that the MEDA programme is planning for Tunisia. Overcrowded public hospitals are being bypassed by private 'multifunctional clinics' that offer better-quality services to those who can afford to pay. There, too, the NGOs and religious associations find they have a role, under the more or less neutral regard of the public authorities, who thus discharge their political obligations more cheaply.

This privatization process has its 'social costs' that are as yet difficult to measure. In certain countries, diseases thought to have been eradicated, such as tuberculosis and malaria, have reappeared, but the dismantling of public prevention structures makes it difficult, if not impossible, to fight the new endemic diseases. It is in this sector that the collapse of the 'social state', inherited from the anti-colonial and developmentalist culture, is most evident. In the agenda of the Barcelona process, it is for these 'collateral' effects of the reform that 30 to 40 per cent of the MEDA budget has been allocated, under the heading 'reinforcing social harmony'.

In the third sector of the Euro-Mediterranean partnership, a large part of the action is left to 'civil society': thousands of humanitarian NGOs have been formed in different countries and their activities are bringing profound changes in the forms of 'social intervention' in the Arab countries. As a result, the figures of the political militant or the trades unionist have lost out and the middle classes have lost relative interest in the political field in its narrower sense, which is shown by their indifference towards, sometimes contempt for, the whole political class. This has also led to widespread demobilization. The economic and social disengagement of the state has therefore resulted in a contraction of the political field, which has been abandoned by 'civil society' to clan struggles for power, as well as to Islamic activism.

The real issues at stake in the Euro-Mediterranean project

During our investigation, we were more and more perplexed about the declared issues of the Barcelona process, both on the part of the EU and on that of the countries south of the Mediterranean. In fact, as compared with Mexico vis-à-vis the United States and Canada, the southern Mediterranean countries play a relatively small role in the general economy of the European Union. The EU is more interested in engaging in central and eastern Europe for carrying out its global strategy and maintaining its position as a leading regional pole for globalization. The direct foreign investment that flows into the two different regions clearly illustrates the preference of European investors for central and eastern Europe, particularly as concerns the oil and gas industry. This is a perfect illustration of the anticipated meagre results of the Euro-Mediterranean partnership.

Some 'critical' analysts of the Barcelona process think that the European strategy is to transform the countries south of the Mediterranean into a huge market for European trade, but that is only a partial aim. This market will always be restricted and it will not grow much larger than the present 3 to 4 per cent of European external trade. Thus it is quite illusory to expect that the Barcelona process will produce more than it has already 'given': that is, a profound restructuring of the Arab economies and societies, according to the logic of the Bretton Woods institutions, with only a little less brutality than their policies in the African countries south of the Sahara. It is no exaggeration to say that the southern Mediterranean countries will become in the future a free trade zone, a marginalized sub-region, heavily dependent on the European Union but also much less developed than its counterparts in the North American and south-east Asian free trade zones. As far as we can see, the interest of the EU in the countries south of the Mediterranean lies elsewhere.

Unfortunately, apart from the relatively small economic interest that the EU has in the countries south of the Mediterranean, the latter find themselves in a most strategic position for the future of the European Union – at least in the present regional and global configuration. This is because of the importance for the Europeans of the immigration issue, as well as of the Israel–Palestinian and Israel–Arab conflicts. The two questions are deeply intertwined, as we shall see later on, even if their causes are very different. It is this position that makes them obligatory 'partners' of the European states and which, according to us, largely justifies the laborious construction of the Barcelona process and the interest the EU is taking in the countries south of the Mediterranean. The events of 9/11 have, indeed, greatly contributed to reinforcing this position.

Immigration and its consequences At the present moment in the EU there are nearly 18 million 'non-nationals'[64] out of 370 million inhabitants – in other words 5 per cent of the total population. Two-thirds are concentrated in three countries: France, Germany and the United Kingdom. Most of them are long-term residents (living there for over ten years). The immigrants come mainly from Turkey (especially in Germany) and from the Maghreb – Morocco, Algeria and Tunisia (especially in France and Spain). Compared with the United States and even other African and Asian countries that receive many more foreigners, Europe is considered to be much more 'closed' to immigration. These immigrants are 'workers', they are between twenty-five and sixty years of age (60 per cent) and most of them are engaged in 'CDE' (demanding, dangerous and dirty activities), for which, in terms of work, salaries and availability, employers do not want nationals who claim too much and are protected by unions – and who often refuse such jobs.

The tradition of immigrant labour goes back to the period of European reconstruction and of the 'Thirty Glorious Years'. It is now recognized that the service that this labour has rendered Europe has been incalculable, making up for its post-war demographic deficit by filling the least well-paid jobs in construction, public works, steelworks and as skilled labour in mechanical construction factories. As from the 1980s, however, Europe gradually closed its borders to this type of immigration. Meanwhile, the law on regrouping families greatly changed the style of living of the immigrants and their families, who settled down on the outskirts of the large cities and sent their children to school there. This increasingly had an impact on the cultural and political character of European societies. The right wing and extreme right have found fertile soil in this development, working on the stereotypes of the European collective imagination to mobilize voters in depressing electoral campaigns incapable of raising any other issues than security. But this gradual closing of the frontiers, which have now become almost water-tight, coincides – for the Arab countries south of the Mediterranean and Turkey – with the arrival on the labour market of a large part of their populations (in 1995, almost 60 per cent of the population between fifteen and sixty-four years). And this population, in its turn, is confronted by unemployment rates of 30 per cent, thanks to liberalization. Emigration, including the clandestine variety, remains for a large majority the only way to salvation.

The demographic decline of Europe (falling birth rate and ageing population) is going to accentuate its labour requirements if it is to maintain its growth but also keep a relative balance between those in active work and the financing of pensions. Who is going to pay our pensions, if not the new immigrants? is being asked on all sides. A report from the population division of the United Nations in 2000 even tried to quantify these needs, which would be around 700 million in the next fifty years. This would mean, for France alone, an average of 1.7 million new immigrants each year. These figures cannot be verified, but labour requirements are now being publicly acknowledged, even by those who resisted them, such as the former prime minister Alain Juppé, notorious for having forcefully evacuated the church of St Bernard in 1995 when it was sheltering people without legal documents (*'sans papiers'*). Today this same politician declares: 'Given the evolution of people's mentalities and taking its demography into account, Europe is going to need foreign labour.'[65]

The demand for work in northern Europe and the offer of work in the southern Mediterranean thus match perfectly and one might have thought that this opportunity would reinforce the solidarity so often proclaimed in the Barcelona process. This is not the case at all. On the contrary, we are seeing the establishment of 'Fortress Europe', with an impressive arsenal of administrative and police arrangements and regulations which are to ensure the water-tightness of the European frontiers. The European security services are undergoing a huge expansion, with the reinforcement of the powers of customs and police officers, the creation of a European judicial area, harmonization of the Schengen procedures, the weakening of controls over expulsion, increasing difficulties in obtaining visas, etc.[66]

The gradual transfer of the immigration issue into the field of internal (national) and regional (European) security is significant. It has been forcefully denounced by human rights associations and some militant politicians but the security drift seems ineluctable. Apart from the important role that the immigrant question plays in electoral campaigns – which partly explains the derailment of the left political parties on this issue – immigration presents two kinds of problems for the European Union, which is still in construction. At the economic and social level, the question cannot be avoided: Europe needs labour, but it does not want uncontrolled immigration that risks becoming permanent. It wants an 'immigrant labour force' but not an 'immigrant society', i.e. one that cannot, or only with difficulty, be integrated culturally and politically.[67] The old immigration policies must thus change and on all sides we hear about 'selective immigration',[68] 'quotas', seasonal contracts, etc. The evident requirements of the European economies are in fact in complete contradiction with the 'ethnic' and political needs of European societies.[69]

Since 9/11 this contradiction has become still more acute. Clandestine immigration having already been 'criminalized', the new anti-terrorist laws, adopted or in the process of being adopted, dramatize the question. The southern Mediterranean countries, the chief source of this labour, which is overwhelmingly Muslim, give the impression of being, paradoxically, the source for renewing the European labour force, at the same time as being zones of 'endemic terrorism'. Controlling the flow of labour, as could be done with any other commodity (it is called 'quality control'), thus becomes a multifaceted strategic issue – related to economics, of course, but also to culture, society and, finally, security.

However, as Marx has already observed, the worker is a social being who must not be confused with the product that he sells, his labour. Hence the European Union, in its infinite need to control everything, has an absolute necessity to 'involve' the southern Mediterranean states, especially the Arab ones. And it is according to their readiness to cooperate in this question (see above) that they will be evaluated and recompensed. For who would be better placed to make a first selection than these state administrations: in terms of skills, but also in establishing 'psychological' and political control of the candidates? Especially as their administrations and police, less concerned than their European counterparts by 'human rights' associations, can carry out more effective controls at the neighbourhood level, thus sparing the EU officials the inconvenience of removing people and the more delicate 'infringement of liberties' that the European laws do not so easily tolerate.

In our view, it is this, the hidden face of the 'Euro-Mediterranean partnership', that truly represents the 'dialogue and cooperation' that was eagerly anticipated as the first plank of the process, i.e. its security and political aspects.

Israel, Palestine, the Arab world: a conflict in Europe The drift of immigration towards becoming a security issue is clearly strongly linked to the Israel–Palestine conflict, now, more than ever before. Since 9/11, but even before that date, when Sharon came to power and there were daily bombardments of Palestinian towns by the Israeli army, the 'European common security policy' has revealed its powerlessness and contradictions. More than ever, the strategy announced so ceremoniously and implemented in the Barcelona process seems to have been a delayed reaction to this important question and the urgent need to resolve it.

It is true that the EU cannot be a rival to the United States in addressing this conflict. And the choice of 'Mediterranean partners' rather than 'Arab partners' should also be seen in the context of this voluntary limitation of its international political role.[70] Thus the strategy defined in the Barcelona consensus appears as it really is: the small part conceded to it by the United States. In other words, it is an illusion that it is possible to treat the integration of Israel into the future free trade zone 'through the economy', while 'dialogue' with Israel is, according to Bistolfi, 'banking on a lasting abandonment of the Arab world in order to forcibly impose – with American support – its military and economic hegemony in the Near East'.[71]

But there is a reasoning behind this 'squaring of the circle'. Israel, being incapable of intervening politically in settling the conflict in spite of its economic and military power, believes that through this low-key strategy it can diminish the intensity of the conflict and, in any case and at all costs, avoid being moved away from the European field by its consequences. With their large Arab and Muslim immigration populations, who have kept strong ties with their countries of origin, the big European cities, also aware of the flagrant injustices inflicted on the Palestinian people, find themselves, willy-nilly, involved in the conflict. The young children of immigrants, born in Europe and who sometimes have European nationality, do not have the 'modest' behaviour of their elders. There has even been, as in their countries of origin but for different reasons, a strengthening of religious practices and Muslim culture in adolescent circles in these populations.

Some analysts have also shown that, compared with the effects of the Gulf War on the European Muslim communities, the second *intifada*, exacerbated by the Israeli atrocities and aggravated by the events of 9/11, has deeply influenced the young immigrants in European cities. But, rather than settling the Israeli–Palestinian conflict – which the American strategy forbids them to do – and thus make it much easier to treat its effects in Europe, the EU Mediterranean strategy appears superficial, reacting to symptoms rather than to causes and, in order to do so, requiring the intervention of states and the civil societies of the southern Mediterranean countries. They believe that, through joint meetings, conferences, Mediterranean forums and juridical constraints created by the association agreements, adversaries can be transformed into partners – or at least they can make people believe that it is possible.

Involving the Arab states of the southern Mediterranean countries is hence of vital importance, getting them to 'trade' with Israel, to establish economic, diplomatic and NGO contacts, to bring together intellectuals and businesspeople in common forums. These are the high-profile measures that have been implemented by the European strategists, but they are designed more to ward off reality than to confront it. They also count on time, the long-term time of economics that eases conflicts and ends by extinguishing them – as had been done, people were given to believe, by the Oslo agreements.

The Arab countries agree to play this game because they have been promoted to the rank of 'partners'. But it also enables them to blame the 'Euromed constraints' for the alignment which they themselves, in spite of the lack of political commitment and the political demobilization of Arab societies, are unable to impose on their own public opinion.

The Barcelona compromise

In his excellent article,[72] Robert Bistolfi ponders on the 'virtuality' of the Euro-Mediterranean project and subtly analyses the illusions it conveys. Carrying his analysis still further, we may pose the question whether the states on both sides of the Mediterranean, particularly the southern states, are not dupes of the virtuality of their project. Are they not aware of the non-correlation between the discourse on partnership and the tough realities of dependence, the predictable marginalization of their societies, and the impossibility of settling the Palestinian question by the measures proposed? Certainly, politics is a cynical business, but this is not quite enough to explain their position. Our hypothesis is that the political leaders and dominant classes of the southern states of the Mediterranean no longer have the legitimacy to govern their respective societies. By displacing their own responsibilities on the 'external factors' responsible for the constraints created by globalization, the necessities of partnership and the opening up of their economies, they can avoid the task of constructing a popular consensus on policies that would call into question their own hold on power. The 'constraints' of globalization and of the 'partnership' of Europe are thus cleverly utilized by local leaders who emphasize their inevitability ('nothing can be done', 'it's this or going backwards', etc.). They assert their own legitimacy as simple 'managers' of the economic deregulation that has been imposed from outside. This gives rise to ambiguity, compromises and attempts at ideological manipulation. Left-wing intellectuals and political militants analyse and denounce the current forms of neoliberal globalization and see the Barcelona process as part of it. But these people can be utilized – and often are – by these same 'managers', who cunningly adopt their counter-discourse to present themselves to public opinion as being 'forced' to comply with them.

This legitimacy has the support of European and global institutions, which seize on the opportunity to evaluate it according to the 'good governance' criteria, established by themselves. Opening up the economy, privatization, etc. are presented as the prerequisites of modernization that will make democratization possible. The leaders who embark on this path are protected by external institutions whose support seems more important than that of internal social and political forces. The Arab leaders cleverly play on these two discourses to justify their actions: Samir Amin amusingly makes the point that they are the 'mamelukes' of our time. With this model, the authoritarianism of governments is tolerated, on the sole condition that they comply with the injunction to open their markets. Thus we have a totally original situation, political authoritarianism coupled with an economic liberalism that enjoys the support of the 'democratic' Western states. This model also has the 'virtue' of accentuating national, or rather nationalist, rivalries between the countries on the southern side of the Mediterranean, thus making autocentric regional dynamics still more difficult.

Morocco is put into competition with Tunisia, the Maghreb with the Mashrek (the eastern Arab states, starting with Egypt). For what counts with the local leaders is to negotiate 'better' contracts than those of their neighbours. The European states are mainly concerned that the southern Mediterranean countries fully adhere to the implementation process and that they involve the 'useful' sectors of their society, particularly the middle classes for which they have fabricated a political and cultural category corresponding perfectly to what they call civil society. Requirements that have since become conditionalities are further formulated by the EU states to push local authorities into respecting the freedoms of association, of the press, multi-partyism, etc. Samir Amin has perceptively analysed the emergence of NGOs and the political issues that this entails[73] in the societies of the Arab world, particularly in Egypt. For Algeria, recent statistics show that, over the last few years, some 36,000 NGOs have been created, which is almost as many as the 40,000 'import-export' businesses set up after the dismantling of the state monopoly over external trade. In fact, the institutionalization of these new political and civil roles is not enough to explain their rapid adoption by the actors concerned and the infatuation that it has created, according to country and period, for fashions in language and behaviour.

For the political leaders, privatization has consisted mainly in the dismantling of the public sector for the benefit of those in power. According to the historical development of each country, the sharing is divided more or less 'equitably' between the dominant families, groups, cliques and clans and is quite consistently carried out according to existing hierarchies, visible or invisible. Political power thus becomes deeply entrenched with 'business' in Algeria, where people talk of the political and financial mafia. In Egypt it is the 'Fardi' sector – but everywhere the process is basically the same. It is the holders of power who help themselves first. In some cases they do not hesitate to eliminate those who resist: in Algeria hundreds of middle-level management state employees have been imprisoned and sometimes physically eliminated.

The EU states and the Bretton Woods institutions, which are taking all precautions for their own interests, do not interfere. Reform follows its course, the public sectors are privatized, states gradually withdraw from commercial activities or from 'trading': what is essential is to carry the process out to the end, thus making it 'irreversible' and all the while linking it with the famous civil society which will 'whitewash' its more sinister aspects.

The Barcelona process is also a process of large-scale 'corruption' of political leaders who are expected to commit themselves more thoroughly to neoliberalism, signing association agreements, getting them adopted by parliaments and obliging the whole technostructure to implement them. Later on, as hushed voices say in the corridors of the European Commission, the new owners, who are incompetent and lazy, will sell out. In any case, the main obstacle to the reform has been removed, more easily than was anticipated. The old ideological antagonists have taken no action; economic interests have prevailed and once again capitalism shows that it functions best without ideology.

However, while the middle classes – or, at least, a section of them – and the ruling classes have got their cut out of the deal – obviously these are social categories and not individuals – what about the popular classes whom the reforms in progress can only 'push towards the bottom'? The new Euro-Mediterranean policy makes it impossible to escape, except on an individual basis, from an irresistible and continuous deterioration of their living standards. As there are no precise data about the forms of resistance they may undertake to arrest the present trends, any conjectures must remain purely speculative.

For the time being, the weak 'alternative' movements, trades unions and democratic associations, are confined in their actions to intellectual and university circles. What mobilization exists is mostly organized by humanitarian and religious associations. Sometimes, as in Algeria, there is a growing tendency for groups in villages or even small towns to set up bodies to monitor public expenditure, the distribution of social housing or European aid money. In Morocco, the associations of the 'young unemployed graduates' intervene in the public recruitment process and act as self-help unions. In Tunisia, the Internet has enabled associations defending human rights to distribute information on the atrocities of the security forces, as well as the corruption accompanying the economic reform process. It is, however, difficult, at the moment, to see any way out of this closed, conflictual structure unless a regional dynamic links up with the international movements that are resisting globalization.

Notes

1 After *The Age of Revolution, The Age of Capital* and *The Age of Empire*, Eric Hobsbawm completes his work with *The Age of Extremes*, in which he paints a comprehensive, fascinating picture of what he calls this 'short twentieth century', the end of which is symbolically marked by the fall of the 'Berlin Wall' and which, far from announcing some 'end of history', opens up a new period of uncertainty.

2 These intellectuals are in no way 'free thinkers' acting within the cultural superstructure, motivated mainly by the development of their ideas. As Keith Dixon, in his short but incisive historical study, has shown, 'think tanks' have been formed and educated in institutions created for this purpose by groups of capitalist interests in the West. They are supported in their tasks by prestigious training centres and their ideas are relayed by the vast international media. The whole thing seems to be a completely coherent system of production and distribution of the 'glorious future' which is called, for the present cycle

of capitalism, globalization. See: Keith Dixon: *Les Evangelistes du marché*, Paris: Liber. Raison d'Agir, 1998. See also an excellent number of the journal *Actes de la Recherche en Sciences Sociales*: 'Les ruses de la raison imperialiste', Paris: Seuil, March 1998.

3 As Pierre Bourdieu has remarked: 'The notion of globalization, which has so many meanings, has the effect, if not the function of imposing, in a kind of cultural ecumenism, the economic fatalism of the effects of imperialism and to make it seem that transnational relationships are a natural necessity.' In *Actes de la Recherche en Sciences Sociales*, Paris: Seuil, no. 121–2, p. 110.

4 Karl Polanyi, *The Great Transformation*, Boston: Beacon Press, 1944.

5 Eric Hobsbawm's *The Age of Extremes* is an impassioned account of this world competition between two systems. But, as the author notes, it is paradoxically the capitalist societies that draw the greatest social benefits from this competition.

6 See the detailed study made by Manuel Castells in *La société en réseau*, Paris: Fayard, 1998, p. 94.

7 Castells, ibid., p. 22.

8 The French historian François Braudel set out to reconstruct the main lines of the capitalist history of the world.

9 Castells, op.cit.

10 Pierre Bourdieu, *Contre-Feux*, Paris: Raisons d'Agir, 1998, p. 67.

11 'The polarization of the "classic" era,' observes Samir Amin, 'was virtually synonymous with the contrast between industrialized and non-industrialized countries. The monopoly of the centres, through which unequal accumulation was reproduced and deepened at the world level, was accomplished through industrialization [...] The polarization which is now at work in the world system is no longer based on the industrial monopoly of the centres alone. The more important peripheries have also, in their turn, entered into the industrial era (although Africa has not really done so). Rather than the old industrial monopoly, there is now what I would call the "five monopolies" of the centres: technological initiative, access to the planet's natural resources, control of globalized finance, communications, weapons of mass destruction. Taken all together, these five monopolies define the form and new content of the globalized law of value on the basis of which accumulation at the world level reproduces and deepens the polarization.'

12 During the 'European Days for the Territorial Representatives of the State', which were held in Paris in 1999, the workshop on the 'State representatives when faced by crises' discussed clandestine immigration, which was felt to be a 'worrying potential source of crisis'. The final report read: 'It is worth mentioning an issue that has already created serious difficulties for many Europeans and will continue to do so: clandestine immigration. All European countries may fear the consequences [...] Regulating immigration, the social integration of immigrants, development assistance and the struggle against the gangs who organize clandestine entry are all serious challenges for the European Union [...] It is essential to be prepared for crisis situations. Public officials and their teams should be trained for action and how to

behave effectively before, during and after a crisis.' See IHSE, *La Documentation française*, Paris, 1999.

13 Commentators agree on the present 'paradox' of the 'globalization' movement. While modern means of transport continue to develop, the number of reception centres for international immigrants has diminished. The result, in developed countries, is that the migratory flows tend to concentrate, thus reinforcing the impression that the phenomenon is rapidly expanding. See *Sciences Humaines*, Paris: occasional paper no. 8, March 1995.

14 Annual Report of the MEDA Programme, 1999. Commission of the European Community, Brussels, 2000, p. 3.

15 Chris Patten, *Barcelona, Five Years Later*, Brussels: European Union publication, 2001.

16 Patten, ibid., p. 7.

17 Patten, ibid., p. 9.

18 Agnès Chevalier: 'Projet euro-méditerranéen et mondialisation', in *Confluences*, no. 21, Spring, 1997.

19 *Towards a New Form of Euro-Mediterranean Partnership*, Institut Català de la Mediterrànià Barcelona, 1995, p. 285.

20 Sébastien Sadek, *Arabies*, no. 168, December 2000.

21 *A New Impetus for the Barcelona Process*, Brussels: European Commission, September 2000.

22 After the adoption of the 'Peace and Stability Charter' it was envisaged that these ad hoc meetings of senior officials should be transformed into an institutional forum for dialogue on policy and security, and mechanisms were to be created to promote effective joint action in the fields of terrorism, conflict prevention and crisis management. Obviously, the second *intifada* outbreak and the 9/11 attacks have postponed the adoption of the charter.

23 *A New Impetus for the Barcelona Process*, op. cit., p. 15.

24 The National Economic and Social Councils theoretically include those responsible for economic, social and cultural institutions (business, social security agencies, hospitals, teachers, etc.), as well as representatives of the state and of personnel (trades unions). They elaborate sectoral studies, which they submit to political leaders but also to public opinion through the media, associations and trades unions.

25 See *Euromed Report*, no. 18, November 2000.

26 *A New Impetus for the Barcelona Process*, op.cit., p. 13.

27 The Islamic charity associations did not await these new developments before intervening in society, sometimes forcefully, in Egypt. The old tradition of foundations – *habous* and *waqf* – thus provided them with a head start over the new NGOs, which were strongly influenced by Western systems in their organization and operations.

28 *Towards a New Scenario for the Euro-Mediterranean partnership*, Institut Català de la Mediterrànià, p. 274.

29 *A New Impetus for the Barcelona Process*, op.cit., p. 14.

30 As formulated by Robert Bistolfi, whose work has already been cited.

31 The European Union has even set up a procedure for providing exper-
tise, the MEDA teams, which enable its Brussels consultants to organize and
manage the activities of the national delegations and thus to ensure that there
is a permanent coming and going between 'the field' and the 'metropolitan
headquarters'.

32 As well as the Arab countries (Syria, Lebanon, Palestine, Jordan,
Egypt, Tunisia, Algeria and Morocco) the southern Mediterranean countries
include Turkey, Malta, Cyprus and Israel, the first three of which aim at being
integrated into the European Union. Israel is in a hostile and dominating
position vis-à-vis the Arab countries. These four states, because of their economic level and history, have very little in common with the Arab states.

33 The embargo on Libya was later lifted.

34 This denial goes to great lengths: in a survey entitled 'The Mediterranean Space' carried out by the Institut Català de la Mediterrànià in 1995,
1,500 questionnaires were sent by post to Euro-Mediterranean personalities
representing civil society (universities, NGOs, private enterprises and public
centres). The form presented two series of questions: one, the imaginary and
the representation of the Mediterranean; two, North–South relationships
– conflicts and cooperation. Languages employed were Catalan, Spanish,
French and English. No comment.

35 The newsletter of the CIRPES (Centre Interdisciplinaire de Recherches
sur la Paix et d'Etudes stratégiques) on 'The strategic debate' observed perceptively: 'The security interests of the Europeans and the Euro-Mediterranean
partnership have been ill served by a strategy that creates relationships
between the Union and the southern side of the Mediterranean but which is
unconnected to the Oslo peace process in the Middle East, managed under
American hegemony.' No. 53, November 2000.

36 We have taken these notions from Jean-Paul Sartre's *Critique de la raison
dialectique*.

37 See the table at the end of the book showing the state of the respective
association agreements of the EU with its southern partners.

38 Ibid.

39 *A New Impetus for the Barcelona Process*, p. 14.

40 Ibid., p. 16.

41 Ibid., p. 16.

42 Some, like the association of the young unemployed graduates in
Morocco, have become strong enough to organize mass demonstrations which
have made the public authorities take their demands into consideration. In
Algeria, a fair number of these young jobless people will be taking to the
maquis to join armed Islamic organizations.

43 UNDP, 1999 Human Development Report.

44 *Population et démographie dans les pays arabes*, Algiers: CNEAP, 2000.

45 *Implementing the MEDA Programme*, Brussels: European Commission,
1998, p. 32.

46 The debt per head of the population is calculated by dividing the total

debt (in 1994), according to the World Bank, by the total population (in 1993), according to the UNDP Human Development Report, 1996.

47 Susan George, op.cit., p. 32.

48 In *Le partenariat euro-méditerranéen vu du Sud,* Paris: L'Harmattan, 2001, p. 30.

49 George, op. cit., p. 54.

50 It is well known that the demographic decline of Europe is going to increase its needs for the immigrant labour necessary to maintain growth and socio-economic balance. Europe will need massive immigration in order to keep its present ratio of active to inactive people at 1:2. This figure would rise to 1:4 if immigrant flows are not increased.

51 *Le partenariat euro-méditerranéen vu du Sud,* Paris: L'Harmattan, 2001, p. 30.

52 George, op. cit., p. 54.

53 Ahmed Dahmani, *EU/Maghreb: dépasser le libre échange, bâtir le partenariat* (cyclostyled document).

54 For further details, see Appendix.

55 *The MEDA Evaluation,* op.cit., p. 51.

56 Ibid., p. 32.

57 Khader, op.cit., p. 51.

58 See *Qu'a-t-on appris de l'Aléna*, Ministère français du territoire et de l'environnement, Paris, July 2000, p. 29.

59 Ridha Gouia, 'Les flux d'investissements étrangers dans les PSM', in *Le partenariat euro-méditerranéen vu du Sud*, op.cit., p. 99.

60 Ibid., p. 98.

61 This is one of the conclusive points made in Ridha Gouia's article, ibid., p. 99.

62 In the case of Mexico, a foreign investor attacked the state on environmental legislation and won the case. The system developed by NAFTA for protecting investors enables them to question environmental protection policies established by the state.

63 Indeed, the 'future' of the new free trade zone can already be read in the recent history of Latin America. 'Privatization in South America has progressed alarmingly, spreading into all sectors, especially those linked to the public services. In Bolivia, few sectors have escaped it: electricity, trains, air transport have been sold off cheaply under pressure from the international financial institutions. The distribution of drinking water and sanitation has also undergone management change towards the private.' In 'Grains de sable', *Courrier d'information d'Attac*, no. 289, December 2001. The strategists of the European Union envisage, for the countries south of the Mediterranean, a convention on water – a rare resource in this region – that would end up by being managed by private companies, particularly European ones. Under the influence of the World Bank and the IMF as well as the Barcelona consensus, the political classes and trade unions in these countries have abdicated their power and accepted the inexorable need to allow private companies (Vivendi,

La Lyonnaise des Eaux, etc.) to take over this natural resource, from the catchment area to distribution. Negotiations are being carried out country by country, although the groundwater is 'regional'.

64 This notion is now very controversial among statisticians in European countries. In France, for example, there is a distinction between 'foreigners' and 'immigrants', in other words people born abroad, some of whom have meanwhile acquired French nationality. Among the 'non-nationals', it is necessary to distinguish immigrants from foreigners, according to the current legislation, between 'territorial law' or 'blood law'.

65 Alain Morice, 'Le travail mondialisé', *Le Monde Diplomatique*, November 2000.

66 See the excellent analysis made by Didier Bigo, 'L'Archipel des polices', in *Le Monde Diplomatique*, October 1996.

67 As Bernard Dréano has noted: 'Parliamentarians and some intellectuals are offended by the "non-integration" of the youth of their country, without understanding that for a long time – alas – part of the youth (and not only Muslim) has undergone a real disintegration, after years of "social treatment" without a mobilization of citizens, in the cities deserted by the parties and trade unions.' In 'Grains de sable', op.cit.

68 The CDU in Germany has finally accepted a 'pilot limitation' project on immigration, with the aim of meeting the economic needs of Germany, which is experiencing an inexorable decline in its active population. The CSU has agreed with the CDU to propose a system of flexible quotas and criteria for selecting immigrants in function of the age and qualifications of candidates.

69 In Greece farmers have been angry when the police arrest immigrants and asked the government to stop these round-ups. However, they also ask the police to escort these workers personally to the frontier at the end of the harvest season. See Morice, op. cit.

70 We say voluntary because, with the exception of a few states like France and Belgium, the great majority, including the United Kingdom and Berlusconi's Italy, are in favour of the American strategy and its world leadership.

71 Robert Bistolfi, 'L'Europe et la Méditerranée, une entreprise virtuelle', *Confluences*, no. 35, autumn 2000, p. 5.

72 Bistolfi, op.cit.

73 See Chapter 1.

4 | On the Euro-Mediterranean partnership

The Arab world fossilized in its powerlessness

In the Arab world, the popular feeling of belonging to one cultural community, if not to one 'nation', in the strict sense of the word, is a reality that has gained strength in the course of the last few decades. One might therefore have expected this sentiment also to serve as the foundation for serious cooperation between the Arab states, or even to motivate these states to embark on the establishment of a kind of political unity (confederate, federal or unitary). Such is not the case; in practice, cooperation/integration is as insignificant in the Arab world as it is in sub-Saharan Africa, for relatively the same reasons and despite the advantage conferred by Arab linguistic unity.

The Arab League, the actual designation of which is the League of Arab States, was modelled on the UNO pattern as an inter-state organization the members of which preserve their full sovereignty, never renounced, even if partially, for the benefit of supranational powers. In this sense, the league is similar to OAU and to the Organization of American States, but not to the European Union.

Should the creation of the league also be viewed as an insipid substitute of Pan-Arabism? In the course of its history, the league has established a series of inter-state specialized Arab organizations modelled on the pattern of the United Nations family, but with modest operational results: many surveys, reports and projects, most of which are of standard quality, but few concrete achievements.

Integration efforts in the region thus assumed other dimensions. In a first phase marked by the triumph of Pan-Arabism in the mid-1950s, as well as the outbreak of the Algerian liberation war until the defeat suffered in the third Israeli–Arab war of 1967, these efforts consisted in attempts to fulfil this unity – even if partially in the beginning – by mobilizing powerful political inputs, one of the landmarks being the creation of the United Arab Republic (1957–1961) from a merger between Egypt and Syria. However, the failure of this form of Arab unification certainly tolled the death-knell of the Nasser/Baathist strategy and gave free rein to the exacerbation of animosity, and even of conflicts, between governments of immediate neighbours (Algeria–Morocco, Syria–Iraq, Saudi Arabia–Yemen and Iraq–Kuwait).

At the same time, as from 1973, the oil manna for some time appeared to replace the radical political will of Pan-Arab populism. This manna was actually accompanied by a large-scale movement of internal migrants from the poor countries (Tunisia, Egypt, Sudan, Palestine, Lebanon, Syria and Yemen) to the rich oil countries (Libya, Iraq and the Gulf countries). Then, when they felt threatened by such 'invasion', the Gulf countries reacted, as already noted, by gradually substituting an immigrant labour force from Pakistan, India and the Philippines. In other respects, the oil manna financed substantial public remittances. However, far from being perceived as the condition sanctioned by the integrative projects, such remittances were generally wasted in the private consumer needs of the ruling classes and in the public consumer needs of the subsidized states. That outcome was completely foreseeable. The ultra-conservative authorities of the Gulf countries act as communication channels of the exigencies of liberal globalization and the hegemonism of the United States, which they have never thought of calling into question. On the contrary, the governments in question have become quasi-protectorates of the United States, in the wake of America's permanent military establishment in the region after the 1990–91 Gulf War. The financial support provided concurrently with the dominant movements associated with political Islam that swear allegiance to the United States gives a negative picture of the effects of the 'oil manna', because political Islam has no interest in Arab unity, hence the call for 'Muslim Ummah' as a substitute for it. In Arabic, there is an untranslatable play on words about this manna with the assertion that the manna (al fawra) has taken the place of the revolution (al thawra). Finally, the oil manna has managed to finance some private investments here and there. But here too, the investments formed part of policies aimed at strengthening parasitic compradors of the middle classes who also do not envisage any future prospects outside liberal globalization.

Under the circumstances, regionalization/integration in the Arab world has failed to make any progress worthy of the name in the course of the last three decades. Like sub-Saharan Africa, the Arab world occupies only subordinate positions in the world system. The volume of its oil exports cannot actually constitute a real substitute for an effective industrialization that can satisfy domestic needs and assist in shaping world markets. As in the case of sub-Saharan Africa (Gabon), there are some 'marginalized rich' countries in the Arab world (the Gulf countries) just as there are many 'marginalized poor' ones. Both groups of countries lack the means to impose themselves as active agents helping to shape the world system. They remain passive agents compelled unilaterally to adapt to the system, even though the region's oil supply might be of vital importance to Western consumers.

The Arab world is therefore living through a phase of its history marked by lack of projects specific to them. It is therefore not surprising that the others take the initiative in making 'proposals', which they impose on their Arab partners.

Thus, the United States of America, which considers the Middle East as a priority region under its exclusive authority (the Europeans being invited just to support its presence in the region) ever since the defunct Soviet Union was discarded, has concocted the Middle East 'common market project', together with Israel and Turkey, its two allies (and with the unconditional support of governments of the Gulf countries). Not only does this project legitimize Israel's expansionist practices in the occupied Palestine relegated to the status of a bantustan; it also offers the Zionist state the advantage of serving as the indispensable financial and technological intermediary between the multinationals and countries in the region. In this context, one can talk of 'regionalization' only in the sense of a North–South project (United States, Israel, Middle East region) operating in the framework and for the benefit of liberal globalization and American hegemonism.

For its part, Europe made qualified proposals for a 'Euro-Mediterranean partnership' that fell within the same logic. Even though this project would already have failed, it did help to deepen the Maghreb–Mashreq cleavage. In fact, by virtue of the agreements on their association with the European Union, the Maghreb countries are more integrated into the European productive system (to which they supply poorly paid sub-contracted products) than the Mashreq countries. The 'sharing of the burden', in the American political jargon, finds expression here in a division of labour that assigns the Middle East and its oil resources to the United States, and the Maghreb and its emigrants to Europe.

The 'Euro-Mediterranean' partnership

Europe and the Arab world are two regions which have maintained complex relations throughout their history on account of their geographic proximity and their common Hellenistic ancestry, from which originated Christianity and Islam. However, the North–South demarcation between 'developed' Europe and the 'under-developed' Arab world, such as we know it, was definitively established only belatedly, with the capitalist expansion reinforced by the colonization of the South segment that recently ended (the British left Egypt only in 1954 and even tried to return there in 1956; the French did not recognize Algeria's independence until 1962).

In the post-Second World War period, relations between Europe and the Arab world came within the dominant logic of the United States' geo-politics and geo-strategy. The North Atlantic Treaty Organization (NATO) actually considered the Arab world as an opponent, while the Soviet Union supported the Arab world's attempts at autonomous development. Having withdrawn from the region, Europe allowed the United States to operate there alone, the support of their loyal allies, such as Turkey, Israel and the governments of the Gulf thus guaranteeing the vital oil supply to Europe.

Was the disappearance of the Soviet antagonist going to herald new prospects for genuine cooperation between the European Union and the Arab world? One might have thought so at one point, when Europe took the initiative in formulating, in Barcelona in 1995, a proposal designated as 'Euro-Mediterranean' partnership. Today, it can be seen that this process is not just 'at a standstill' but that it has collapsed.

This collapse came about because the project had been designed on the basis of an unacceptable and incredible principle and could therefore not be implemented, even if some of its promoters might well have been well-intentioned partners. The European partner is now rallying not only the Mediterranean Europeans, but all the countries of the European Union. It is a right for Europeans, which nobody can call into question (the right to think of sharing common interests and of having to contemplate a common future). This is an indisputable right for all Europeans, even if those in each of the concerned countries also have the right to criticize (as some people do) the European project as it stands today.

The other partner is curious; it is composed of all the riparian entities along the south and east coast of the Mediterranean. However, the majority of these riparian elements happen to be Arab countries that also belong to a distinct world: the Arab entity. Whether a nationalistic Arab or not, this world exists and it should therefore be recognized that the Arab world might have certain common tendencies, a certain sense of common interest and a common vision of its integration into the contemporary world. Separating the Mediterranean Arab countries from the non-Mediterranean Arab countries is actually unacceptable. What is needed is therefore a Euro-Arab agreement – in other words, an agreement between all the European countries and all the Arab, regardless of whether they are Mediterranean or not. The Mediterranean concept is meaningful only if entails rallying all the riparian countries around problems concerning the common sea, for instance in the area of pollution. It is not on this narrow basis that one can contemplate the future of relations between Europe and this small portion of the South known as the Arab world.

On the other hand, the era of the Barcelona Conference (1995) was also that of the Madrid and Oslo Conferences, that is, a period when a certain type of peace between Arabs and Israel was being promoted under the leadership of the Americans. In this way, the Europeans implemented a strategy complementary to that of the United States and Israel, aimed at dictating the content of the said peace, a kind of peace imagined on a basis that should have been perceived in advance as unacceptable, since it was equivalent to the establishment of a bantustan – there could not be a better term – in the occupied territories of Palestine.

It is at this moment and in this geographical context that the Euro-Mediterranean project was contemplated. It consisted in using the new international economic situation to impose on the Arabs Israel's integration into the region and posing as a condition for cooperation between Europe and the Arab countries a similar cooperation between the Arab countries themselves and Israel. By comparison, it is a little as if, in the apartheid era, Europe had forced the African states to regularize their diplomatic and other relations with South Africa as a condition for the support and cooperation the Europeans were offering them.

As an apartheid country, Israel has been implementing a policy of systematic ethnic purgation. It is unacceptable to tolerate Israel, let alone support it. Israel should be boycotted by all civilized countries of the world.

At present, the tragedy developing in Palestine calls for a strong international political intervention accompanied by effective measures for a serious boycott of Israel until the state recognizes the State of Palestine. Europe intervened clamorously in Kosovo to defend a lesser cause than that of Palestine, but it allows the government of Israel to be entrusted to a genuine war criminal who has personally proclaimed his rejection of the Madrid and Oslo agreements! It is true that in the case of Yugoslavia, Europe only stood by a decision previously taken in Washington. On the contrary, in taking an autonomous stand on Palestine, Europe has to distance itself from the United States, which is obviously problematic. This also proves that political Europe does not exist.

The so-called European proposals for 'Euro-Mediterranean partnership' also include an economic component about which the European institutions claimed to have made 'new efforts' in qualifying their proposals as coming within the framework of 'mutual development', 'partnership' and 'joint development', in place of 'aid', a devalued term.

An analysis of these 'partnership' proposals shows that they are nothing of the sort. All these proposals come within the exclusive logic of globalized neoliberalism (opening markets, creating 'enabling' conditions for foreign investment, deregulating and defusing protections, etc.) as formulated by the United States, the WTO, the World Bank and the IMF. Submission to the rules defined by these authorities, including the so-called Structural Adjustment Programmes, is moreover formulated as a pre-condition for implementation of the European proposals. Here too, the real position of Europe is not different from that of the United States. In both their political and economic dimensions Europe's proposals currently form part of a dominant twofold alignment: liberal globalization and United States' hegemonism. The two elements are interrelated. Accepting the exclusive logic of liberal globalization means assigning priority or exclusive importance to the interests of dominant capital. At any rate, the interests of European dominant capital are not fundamentally different from the interests of North American dominant capital. Of course, there are conflicts, but they are common mercantile conflicts of the same kind as the conflicts that can crop up between multinationals of a given country. Europe's possible autonomy vis-à-vis the United States cannot be assumed on this basis.

Other conditions are also imposed by the European partner. Is the reference to respect human rights as a theoretical condition of the partnership agreements desirable? Certainly, even if signed by governments that do not intend to implement its provisions, a charter can become a lever that can be utilized by victims of a system. However, this instrument will at best remain marginal because the struggle for democracy is pre-eminently the people's affair, which must be managed in the concerned country itself. Internationalism in this field is very useful, but it is mainly through internal struggles and the mobilization of democratic forces within societies that change can be fostered. What the external entity can do is precisely to support them and not to fight them.

However, the use that the Great Powers (Europe in this case) intend to make of such interventions in the name of democracy remains dubious. The examples of 'double standards' – which are numerous and obvious – show that this type of utilization is absolutely cynical: the tool is mobilized against an opponent to be weakened but it is put away in the face of an ally. Moreover, the dominant concept at present is that of good governance, to use the jargon in fashion; in other words, the concept of acceptable governability. Alas, this is a poor concept that limits democracy to multi-party systems, formal elections and respect for a number of individual elementary rights, without recognizing social, individual and collective rights, the right to work, education, health and freedom of movement within and outside one's own country. Yet the rights constitute a whole set comprising inseparable elements. If they are not accompanied by the other rights, then political rights become instruments that can be and are manipulated and therefore undermine the cause of democracy, since they destroy its credibility among the people themselves.

Appendix: Basic data on the Arab world

Population data

Population (millions of inhabitants)

1960	92.4
1994	236.0
2000	272.4
Gross mortality rate	0.8

Population growth (%)

1960–94	2.8
1994–2000	2.4
Year the population doubled	2023
Gross birth rate	3.3

Human Development

Human Development Index (HDI)

Life expectancy (yrs)	62.9
Adult literacy (%)	54.7
Rate of schooling, at any level of education (% of 6- to 23-year-olds)	58.0
Gross Domestic Product per inhabitant	$4,450

Gender-specific Index of Human Development (GSHDI)

Life expectancy (years)	female	64.8
	male	62.0
Adult literacy % of pop.	female	40.6
	male	66.9
Schooling, all levels % of pop.	female	53.7
	male	63.3
Percentage share of household income	female	21.7

Classification of Arab countries according to Human Development Index (HDI)

Five Arab countries with high levels of human development (HDI 0.800–0.870)

Bahrein, United Arab Emirates, Libya, Kuwait, Qatar

Eleven Arab countries with average levels of human development (HDI 0.530–0.794)

Algeria, Morocco, Saudi Arabia, Oman, Egypt, Palestine,* Iraq, Syria, Jordan, Tunisia, Lebanon
* Classification according to GNP/inhab., due to absence of classification by UNDP

Six Arab countries with low levels of human development (HDI 0.319–0.412)

Comores, Somalia, Djibouti, Sudan, Mauritania, Yemen

Health

Human Development Index (HDI)

Life expectancy (yrs)	1966	45.5
	1994	62.9
Access to health services (%)	1985–87	77.0
	1994	87.0
Access to drinking water (%)		76.0
Access to sanitation (%)		52.0
One-year-old children vaccinated (%)		
against tuberculosis		93.0
against measles		83.0
Births followed up by health workers (%)		58.0
Weight insufficiency in children		
under 5 years of age (%)	1975	20.0
	1995	14.0
Child mortality (%)	1960	16.6
	1995	6.7
Cases of tuberculosis (per 100,000 inhab.)		41
Cases of malaria (per 100,000 inhab.)		89
Cigarette consumption/adult (base 100 in 1970)		153
Number of inhabitants/medical doctor (1994)		1,516
Disabled persons (%)		2
Health expenditure as % of GDP	1960	0.9
	1986	1.8
	1990	2.9

Food Security

Index of food production/inhab. (base 100 in 1979–81)	121
Daily calories intake/inhabitant	2,874
Food resources from fishery/year/inhab.	5 kg
Import of cereals (in thousands of tons)	34,873

Education and access to communication

Education

Rate of schooling (%)	58
Public expenditure for education (% of GDP, 1980)	4.1
Adult literacy rate (%) 1985	53.0
1994	54.7

Access to communication

Radios per 1,000 inhab.	259
TV sets per 1,000 inhab.	120
Daily newspaper distribution per 1,000 inhab.	45
Books published per 100,000 inhab.	4
Telephone lines (contracts) per 1,000 inhab.	46
Fax machines per 1,000 inhab.	1

Urbanization

Urban population as % of total population	1960	31
	1994	52
	2000	55
Yearly growth rate of total pop.	1960–94	0.046
Population in urban areas of more than 750,000 inhab.		
% of total population		20
of urban population		40

Employment

Total active population (%)		33
Active female population (%)	1970	23
Population active in agriculture (%)	1960	71
	1990	37
Population active in industry (%)	1960	11
	1990	22
Population active in service sector (%)	1960	18
	1990	42

Economy

GDP 1994 in billion $		607
GDP/inhab. 1994 ($)	1988	1,820
	1994	1,978
Annual growth rate of GDP (%)		+2
Annual growth rate of GDP/inhab. (%)	1965–80	+3.8
	1980–93	–0.4
Real GDP/inhab. 1994 ($)		4,450
Evolution of income/inhab. (in $ of 1987)	1960	989
	1970	1,893
	1980	2,757
	1990	1,740
	1994	1,595

Natural resources

Total surface (1,000 ha.)	1,201
Forest and woodland (%)	5.9
Arable land (%)	4.4
Irrigated land (% of arable land)	18

Electricity

Consumption of electricity (in million Kwh)		285,262
Consumption of electricity (base 100 in 1970)		1,233
Consumption of electricity/inhab. (Kwh)	1970	205
	1994	1,229

Oil and natural gas

Proven oil reserves (in billion $)	507.7
% of world total reserves	60.9
Oil production in 1993 (% of world total)	27.5
Oil exports (% of world exports)	40.1
Proven reserves of natural gas (Gm3)	29,517
% of world total reserves	21.0
Gas production in 1993 (% of world production)	11.8
Gas exports (% of world exports)	12.4

Domestic trade 1992

Imports ($m)	120,038
Exports ($m)	140,969
Trade volume ($m)	267,007

The total balance of trade is positive but total balance
of trade in foodstuffs is negative

Imports of foodstuffs	15% of total imports
Exports of foodstuffs	2.6 % of total exports
Trade deficit in foodstuffs ($b)	146.2

Direct investments in the Mediterranean region (in millions $)

	1987–92 yearly av.	1993	1994	1995	1996	1997	1998
Algeria	–	–59	22	–24	447	630	500
Cyprus	83	83	75	119	259	175	200
Egypt	806	493	1,256	598	636	891	1,076
Israel	187	429	355	1,306	1,389	1,455	1,839
Lebanon	2	7	23	22	64	150	230
Malta	46	56	152	183	325	128	130
Morocco	203	491	551	332	354	1,079	258
Syria	67	176	251	100	89	80	100
Tunisia	160	562	432	264	238	339	650
Turkey	578	636	608	885	722	805	807
		2,840	3,728	3,798	4,539	6,093	6,013

Source: CNUCED

Direct foreign investment in the Mediterranean region (in % of gross capital formation)

	1987–92 yearly av.	1993	1994	1995	1996	1997
Algeria	–	–0.5	0.2	–0.2	3.6	5.1
Cyprus	6.5	5.6	4.9	7.0	15.0	10.6
Egypt	4.4	5.3	11.9	5.3	5.1	6.1
Israel	1.8	2.9	2.1	6.4	6.2	6.9
Jordan	1.8	–1.8	0.1	0.7	0.8	20.3
Lebanon	0.5	0.4	1.8	1.5	4.3	10.8
Malta	7.4	7.8	19.1	17.8	34.0	15.0
Morocco	3.8	8.1	8.8	4.7	5.0	15.6
Syria	1.4	1.8	1.9	0.7	0.6	0.6
Tunisia	5.8	13.7	10.2	6.1	5.3	7.3
Turkey	2.0	1.3	1.9	2.2	1.6	1.6

Source: CNUCED

MEDA commitments in 1998 (in €)

General data

Competitive conversion of businesses (BEI)	45,000,000
Integrated rural development/resource management	28,400,000
Support for youth and sport	6,000,000
Support for the health sector	20,000,000
Support for the agency for the normalization/regularization of telecommunications	5,000,000
Support for privatization	5,000,000
Creation of a fund of guarantee	30,000,000
Integrated development of forest areas (northern Morocco)	24,000,000
Primary education	40,000,000
Normal/quality	15,500,000
Total	218,900,000

Morocco – indicative programme 1996–98

Sector/programme	€m	%
Structural adjustment	120.00	26.40
1 – Programme of structural adjustment	120.00	
Support for economic transition	138.50	30.47
2 – Risk capital (BEI)	45.00	
3 – Support for professional training	38.00	
4 – Fund of guarantee	30.00	
5 – Normalization and quality management	15.50	
6 – Support for privatization	5.00	
7 – Support for ANRT	5.00	
Reinforcement of social equity	195.98	43.12
8 – Water and sanitation in rural areas	40.00	
9 – Roads and thoroughfares in rural areas	30.00	
10 – Integrated rural development	28.40	
11 – Support for primary health care	20.00	
12 – Support for primary education	40.00	
13 – Support for youth and sport	6.00	
14 – Integrated development of forest areas	24.00	
15 – Bonus payments for BEI loans	7.58	
Total PIN 1996–98	454.48	100

Egypt: indicative national programme (updated 1997–99)

	millions (€)	%	Observations
Support for economic transition			
Industrial modernization programme	250	33.11	Adopted by the 44th MED committee on 15 September 1998, specific financing convention signed in December 1998.
Development of the financial market	30	3.97	Action likely to be postponed until MEDA II
Professional/management training	60	7.95	Preparation in progress (committee MED 1999)
Subtotal 1	340	45.03	
Support to socio-economic stability			
Social fund for development (phase II)	1,055	20.53	Adopted by the MED committee on 16 July 1997 – specific financing convention signed on 14 April 1998
Programme for primary education	100	13.25	Adopted by the MED committee on 26 September 1996 – specific financing convention signed on 14 April 1998
Support for the programme of reform of the health sector	110	14.57	Adopted by the 44th MED committee on 15 September 1998 specific financing convention signed in December 1998
Subtotal 2	365	48.34	
Environment			
Environment	50	6.62	Bonus for interest payments to the BEI 30.38 million € committed:
			– Water treatment Cairo II (7,07 m€)
			– Water Gabal El Asfar (10 m€)
			– Anti-pollution (2,81 m€)
			– Grey Cement (2,7 m€)
			– Gas pipeline project GASCO (7.8 m€)
Subtotal 3	50	6.62	
Total	755		

Tunisia – indicative programme 1996–98

Sector/programme	Million €	%
Structural adjustment	180.00	50.4
1 – Support for economic reform (FAS I)	100.00	
2 – Support for economic reform (FAS II)	80.00	
Support for economic transition	99.00	27.7
3 – Professional training (MANFORM)	45.00	
4 – Risk capital restructuring	15.00	
5 – Risk capital privatization	15.00	
6 – Support for privatization	10.00	
7 – Support for the competitiveness of the Tunisian economy	10.00	
8 – Promotion of foreign investments (FIPA)	4.00	
Reinforcement of social stability	77.90	21.8
9 – Integrated rural development (DRI/GRN)	50.00	
10 – Support for job creation	9.60	
11 – Cleaning operation Lake Sud: bonus of interests	9.25	
12 – Cleaning operation ONAS III: bonus of interests	9.05	
Total PIN 1996–98	356.90	109

Algeria – indicative programme 1996–98

Sector/programme	Million €	%
Structural adjustment	30.00	22.1
1. Facilitating structural adjustment (a total of 125 million € (of which 95 million € are left over from the financial protocols)	30.00	
Support for economic transition	105.75	77.9
2. Bonus of interests 'programme against industrial pollution'	10.75	
3. Support for small and medium-size business	57.00	
4. Support for industrial restructuring and privatization	38.00	
Total PIN 1996–98	135.75	100

Distribution of successive commitments and payments

The ratio of actual payments to commitments shows considerable differences between countries.

Distribution of MEDA commitments and actual payments per country
MEDA 1 (1995–99) – bilateral and regional cooperation

	Commitment million €	Payment million €	Ratio of actual payment to commitments (%)
Algeria	164	30	18.2
Morocco	656	127	19.4
Tunisia	428	168	39.3
Egypt	686	157	22.9
Jordan	254	108	42.5
Lebanon	182	1	0.5
Syria	99	0	0.0
Turkey	375	15	4.0
West Bank and Gaza	111	54	48.6
Bilateral cooperation	2,955	660	22.3
Regional cooperation 3*	480	230[†]	48
Total	3,435	890	26

* Includes commitments between 1997 and 1999 for a total of 63 million euros for technical assistance by the MEDA teams.
[†] Includes commitments worth approx. 150 million euros in terms of horizontal cooperation agreed to before 1996.

MEDA democracy programme: distribution of the funds

The following table presents the distribution of the funds by four criteria: the beneficiary country, the objectives concerned, the used instruments and the operators responsible for the implementation of the operations.

Beneficiary countries	1996 9,000,000 €		1997 8,000,000 €		1998 10,075,000 €		1999 10,075,000 €	
	%	No. of operations	%	No. of operations	%	No. of operations	%	No. of operations
Morocco	2	19	12	4.5	2	–		
Algeria	5	6	8	5	10.9	5		
Tunisia	0	1	1	1	4.2	1		
Egypt	3	2	6	3	5.9	3		
Jordan	4	3	3	2	7.2	4		
Lebanon	6	4	4	2	5.9	4		
Syria	0	0	3	2	3.9	2		
Palestinian Authority	27	12	12	7	14.9	9	11.3	1
Israel	2	1	7	4	10.9	5	17.2	1
Cyprus	1	1	0	0	0	0	17.2	1
Turkey	2	1	2	1	3.5	1	6.3	1
Malta	0	0	0	0	0	0		
Regional	20	11	30	12	24.6	12	48.0	2
Conflict resolution	26	18		5	2	3.6	2	
	100	62	100	53	100	50	100	6
Concerned objectives (%)								
Democracy	6		15		1			
Rule of law	1		14		13		22	
Civil society	32		28		14		37	

Fundamental freedoms	8	1	24	41
Trades unions	6	4	0	
Vulnerable groups	8	19	23	
Education	11	14	17	
Conflict resolution	29	5	8	
	100	100	100	100
Used instruments (%)				
Education	9	7	5	
Training	16	38	16	22
Awareness raising	73	48	63	45
Network	2	7	16	33
	100	100	100	100
Operators (%)				
Institutions	4	9	3	
European NGOs	26	35	42	48
NGO Mediterranean partners	70	54	54	52
International organizations	0	2	1	
	100	100	100	100

Structural adjustment and privatization

Support for structural adjustment in the framework of the MEDA programme

	Year of adoption	Amount (million €)	Progress by the end of 1998
Morocco	1996	120	1st and 2nd instalments (resp. 30 and 40 million euro) paid in 1997 and 1998
Algeria	1996	125*	1st instalment paid in 1998 (60 million euro)
Jordan	1996	100	Programme completed. 1st instalment (60 million euro) paid in 1996 and 2nd instalment (40 million euro) paid in 1997.
Tunisia –FAS I	1996	100	Programme completed. 1st instalment (40 million euro) paid in 1996 and 2nd instalment (60 million euro) paid in 1997.
Tunisia –FAS II	1998	80	The MED committee has unanimously given positive advice in December 1998; the financing convention should be signed in the 1st semester of 1999.

* Of which 95 million euros from the funds agreed on under the protocol.

Outcome of privatizations in Tunisia 1987–31/03/2000

Period/parameters	1987–91	1992–94	1995–99	Total
Closures (MD)	131	64	1,073	1,268
Concerned firms	38	10	90	138
Number of operations	65	35	192	292

Source: Ministry of Economic Development

The association agreements

Evolution of negotiations relating to the agreements of Euro-Mediterranean Association

Partner	End of negotiations	Signing of the agreement	Date of application
Tunisia	June 1995	July 1995	March 1998
Israel	September 1995	November 1995	June 2000
Morocco	November 1995	February 1996	March 2000
PLO (for the Palestinian Authority)	December 1996	February 1997	July 1997
Jordan	April 1997	November 1997	–
Egypt	Negotiations completed in June 1999	–	–
Lebanon	Negotiations in progress	–	–
Algeria	Negotiations in progress	–	–
Syria	Negotiations in progress	–	–

Sources and bibliography

The following documents are in Arab language. The titles are shown in English translation.

Important publications by the ARC (Cairo)

M. Abu Mandur (ed.), *Impoverishment in Egypt*, 265 pages, 1998.

Ahmad Abdallah (ed.), *Parliamentary Elections in Egypt*, 1990.

Samir Amin, *A Critique of the Soviet and the National Populist State*, 1992.

— (ed.), *State and Civil Society in Egypt*, 1996.

— *State and Civil Society in Lebanon and Mashreq Countries*, 1996.

— (ed.), *State and Civil Society in Maghreb Countries*, 1997.

Adel Chaban (ed.), *Workers in the Struggle for Change*, 1994.

Abdel Ghaffar Chukr, *Islamic NGOs in Egypt*, 280 pages, 2000.

— (ed.), *The Renewal of the Egyptian Progressive Movement*, 69 pages, 2000.

— *NGOs Facing the Economic and Social Crisis in Egypt*, 1997.

Essam Dessouki (ed.), *Workers and Students in the Egyptian National Movement*, 1997.

Shahida El Baz, *Arab NGOs on the Eve of the XXIst Century*, 298 pages, 1997.

Ahmad Nabil el Hilali (ed.), *The Egyptian Left, Its Evolution*, 1992.

— *Political Alliances in Egypt*, 1994.

Farouk El Kadi, *The Knights of Hope*, 2000 (history of the student movement in Egypt).

Ahmad Hassan (ed.), *The Peasant Question*, 1992.

Haydar Ibrahim, *The Crisis of Political Islam in Sudan*, 1990.

Azza Khalil (ed.), *Street Children in the Arab World*, 262 pages.

— *Childhood policies and services in Egypt*, 187 pages, 1999.

— *Women, Poverty and Marginalisation in Egypt*.

Hassanein Kishk (ed.), *Informal Women's Labour*, 100 pages, 2000.

Amina Rachid, *Academic and Social Rights in Egypt*, 358 pages, 1999.

Helmi Shaarawi (ed.), *Human Rights in the Arab World*, 1994.

Helmi Shaarawi, Rouchdi Saïd, Saad El Tawil, Abdel Wahab Amer, Mohamad Sid Ahmad, Ali El Tom, *Water Crisis in the Arab World*, 1999.

Various authors (history of the communist movement), *Testimonies*, 5 volumes to this day, more expected.

Various authors, *Women and Education*, 1992.

Ismail Zakzouk (ed.), *The Marginalized Between Growth and Development*, 49 pages, 1999.

Safaa Zaki Mourad (ed.), *Women in the Textile Industry*, 263 pages, 1999.

Other research and publications

Abd El Basset Dardour, *Political Violence in Algeria and Crisis of Democratic Transformation*, Cairo: Al Amin, 1992.

Abd El Ghani Abo Hany, *Morocco: The Development Model Crisis*, Cairo: ARC, 1997.

Abd El Kader Zghal, *Civil Society and Conflict for Hegemony*, Beirut: Arab Unity Centre, 1992.

Abd El Nasser Gabi, *A Commentary on Abd El Kader Zghal's Previous Research*, Nakd No. 6, March 1994.

Ahmed Balabaky, *Social Development and the State Role, Sociological Observations on the Concept of Human Development*, Beirut: Lebanon Association of Sociology, 1995.

Ahmed Hanni, *On Procedures of Economic Reform in Algeria*, Cairo: ARC, 1988.

Ahmed Thabet, *The Political Cultural Role in Civic Sector*, Cairo: El Ahram Centre for Strategic and Political Studies, 2000.

Ali Bou Anaka, *The State and Ruling Nature in Algeria*, Beirut: Arab Unity Centre, 1997.

Ali el Kenz, *Algeria: Searching for New Social Bloc*, Cairo: ARC, 1997.

Al Monsef Wannas, *The State and Cultural Life in the Maghreb*, Tunis, 1991.

— *Societal Phenomena in the Arab Maghreb*, Tunis, 1997.

— *The National State and Civil Society in Algeria*, Beirut, 1996.

— *In Terms of Confidence Building between NGOs and Their Direct Partners, State Private Sector and World Organizations*, Cairo, May 1997.

Amani Kandel and Sara Ben Nafesa, *Non Governmental Organizations in Egypt*, Cairo: El Ahram Centre for Strategic and Political Studies, 1994.

— *Democratic Transformations Process in Egypt (1981–1993)*, Cairo: Dar El Amin, 1995.

— 'Third Sector in the Arab World', in *Citizens, Civil Society Promotion in the World*, Seficos: Citizen Participation World Alliance, Cairo, 1995.

Arous el Zobeir, *Islamic-Oriented Societies in Algeria*, Cairo: ARC, 1999.

— *Societal Sector in Algeria*, Arab League, 2000.

Atea Huseen Afandi, *Partnership Between State and Civil Society in the State, NGOs and Private Sector*, Beirut: ESCWA, 1999.

ESCWA, Workshop on 'Partnership Between State and Civil Society in Context of World Conferences Commitments, Implementations, Follow up', Beirut, 1990.

Hassan al Bargouty, *Civil Society Organizations in Palestine*, Cairo: ARC, 2000.

Haydar Ibrahim, *Civil Society and Democratic Transformations in Sudan*, Cairo: Ibn Khaldon Centre, 1996.

Hoda Meetkis, 'The Democratic Development in the Arab Maghreb', *Al Ahram*, 1995.

— *The Religious Trend in Morocco*, 1995.

Ibn Khaldon Centre for Development Studies, *Civil Society and Democratic Transformations in the Arab World*, Cairo: Dar El Amin, 1997 and 1999.

Ibrahim Awad, *Economic Crisis, Protestation and Democratic Development: Comparative Study between Algeria and Jordan*, Cairo University, 1993.

Kareem Sobhy (ed.), *Workshop on Arab Trade Unions*, Cairo: Ibn Khadon Centre for Development Studies, 1996.

Mohamed El Harmasy, *The Society and the State in Morocco*, Beirut: Arab Unity Centre, 1987.

Mohamed Tozi, *The Associative Fabric in Morocco*, unpublished, 2000.

Niveen Mossaad, *Political Violence of Religious Social Movements*, Cairo University, 1993.

Onsor Al Aiadhi, *Democracy and Sociology of Rebellion in Algeria*, Cairo: ARC, 1999.

Saied Ben Saied El Alewy et al., *Civil Society in the Arab world and Its Roles in Democratic Practices*, Beirut: Arab Unity Research Centre, 1992.

Other research concerning Egypt

Abdulla, A. (ed.), *Lessons of 1987 Parliamentary Elections in Egypt*, Cairo: Arab Research Centre, 1990.

Abdullah, A., *The Right to Participate and Dialogue Duty*, Cairo: Cairo Centre for Human Rights Studies, 1996.

Abdullah, I. S. et al., *Studies of Arab Progressive Movement*, Beirut: Centre for Arab Unity Studies, 1987.

Abdullah, Th. F., *Mechanisms of Democratic Change in the Arab World*, Beirut: Centre for Arab Unity Studies, 1997.

Abdul-Mageid, W., *Egyptian Political Parties from Inside*, Cairo: Dar Al-Mahrousa, 1993.

Abdul-Moty, A., *Globalization and Societal Transformations in the Arab World*, Cairo: Arab Research Centre, 1999.

Abdul Razek, H., *Normalization and Resisting the Zionist Invasion*, Cairo: Dar Sotour, 2000.

Abu-Taleb, H. and A. Menesy, *Lebanese Elections and Beyond*, Cairo: Al-Ahram Centre for Political and Strategic Studies, 2000.

Ashmawy, S., *Peasants and Authority: Egyptian Peasantry Movements (1919–1999)*, Cairo: MERIT, 2001.

Centre for Trades Unions and Workers Services, *Egyptian Labour in the Last Five Years*, Cairo, 2000.

Committee for Defending National Culture, *From Resisting Normalization to Confronting Hegemony (1979–1994)*, Cairo: Arab Research Centre, 1994.

Douval, A. and A. Hassan (eds), *The Civil Project in Sudan: Questions of Transition on into Democracy and Peace*, Cairo: Centre for Sudanese Studies.

El-Baz, Sh., *Arab NGOs: An Analytical Map*, Unpublished Paper, Cairo: Arab Research Centre, 2000.

El-Gammal, M. M. (ed.) *Palestine and the Arab World*, Cairo: Arab Research Centre, 2001.

El-Gammal, M. M. and Y. Mostafa, *Political Organizations in Egypt*, Unpublished Paper, Cairo: Arab Research Centre, 1996.

El-Khouly, O. A. (ed.), *The Arabs and Globalization*, Beirut: Centre for Arab Unity Studies, 1998.

El-Sayed, M. K. (ed.), *Reality of Political Pluralism in Egypt*, Cairo: Arab Research Centre, 1996.

Farouk, A., *Unions and Constitutional Evolution in Egypt (1923–1995)*, Cairo: Almosada Al-Kanonia Centre for Human Rights, 1997.

Ghalyon, B., *Arab Turmoil: The State Versus the Nation*, Beirut: Centre for Arab Unity Studies, 1993.

Hassan, A. H., *Political Islamic Rising in Professional Syndicates*, Cairo: Al-Dar Al-Thakafia, 2000.

— *Islamic Political Groups and Civil Society*, Cairo: Al-Dar Al-Thakafia, 2000.

Hassan, B. E. (ed.), *Freedom of the Press from a Human Rights Perspective*, Cairo: Cairo Centre for Human Rights Studies, 1995.

Hassan, E. M. (ed.) *Renewing Political Thought on the Lines of Democracy and Human Rights*, Cairo: Cairo Centre for Human Rights Studies, 1995.

— *Pseudo Multi-Party System*, Cairo: Al-Mosada Al-Kanonia Centre for Human Rights, 1999.

— (ed.), *Diaries of Al-Aqsa Intifada*, Cairo: Cairo Centre for Human Rights Studies, 2000.

Hassan, I. M., *Functions of Political Parties in Restricted Pluralism: Al-Tagamu Party Case (1976–1991)*, Cairo: Kitab Al-Ahaly, 1995.

Helal, A., *Arab Nation Security: Challenges of the Coming Decade*, Amman: Arab Thought Forum, 1986.

— *Development of the Political System in Egypt (1803– 1997)*, Cairo: Centre for Political Studies and Research, Cairo University, 1997.

Helal, A. and N. Mosaad, *Arab Political Systems: Questions of Continuity and Change*, Beirut: Centre for Arab Unity Studies, 2000.

Hewedy, A., *Militarization and Security in the Middle East: Their Impacts on Development and Democracy*, Cairo: Dar Al-Shorouk, 1991.

Ibraheim, S. E., *Concerns of Minorities in the Arab World*, Cairo: Ibn Khaldoun Centre for Development, 1994.

Ibrahiem, H., *Civil Society and Democratic Transformation in Sudan*, Cairo: Ibn Khaldoun Centre for Development, 1996.

Ibrahim, S. E., *Arab Civic Magazines*, Cairo: Ibn Khaldoun Centre for Development, 1996.

Kandiel, A., *The Process of Democratic Transformation in Egypt (1981–1993)*, Cairo: Ibn Khaldoun Centre for Development, 1995.

— *Non-Governmental Action and Social Change*, Cairo: Al-Ahram Centre for Political and Strategic Studies, 1998.

— *Civil Society in Egypt and the New Millennium*, Cairo: Al-Ahram Centre for Political and Strategic Studies, 2000.

Land Centre for Human Rights, *Peasant Rights in Egypt: Neglected Cases*, Cairo, July 2000.

— *Labour Protests: Outcry against the Government*, Cairo, 2000.

— *Labour Protests in Egypt: Flash in the Darkness of Crisis*, Cairo, 2000.

Matar, G. and A. Helal, *The Arab Regional Order: A Study of Political Arab Relations*, Beirut: Center for Arab Unity Studies, 1979.

Monieb, M., *Democracy in Egypt: An Unknown Fate*, Cairo: Egyptian Organization for Human Rights, 1996.

Morkos, S., *The West and the Religious Question in the Middle East: Protection and Punishment*, Cairo: MERIT, 2000.

Moustafa, H., *Political System and the Questions of Democratic Transformation in Egypt*, Cairo: MERIT, 1999.

Nasief, E., *Land Lease Relations: National Issue*, Cairo: Dar Al-Thakafa Al-Gededa, 1999.

Rashwan, D., *Changes in the Islamist Groups in Egypt*, Cairo: Al- Ahram Centre for Political and Strategic Studies, 2000.

Sabour, I., *Knowledge and Authority in Arab Society*, Beirut: Centre for Arab Unity Studies.

Said, M. S., *Prospects of Arab Regional Order After the Crisis in the Gulf*, Kuwait: Alam El-Marefa, 1992.

Samak, N. A., *NGOs and the Economic Development in Egypt*, Cairo: Centre for the Study of Developing Countries, 1999.

Sayegh, A. (ed.), *The Arab Intellectual: His Concerns and His Giving*, Beirut: Centre for Arab Unity Studies, 1995.

Sharawy, H., *Dialogues with Samir Amin*, Beirut: Kanaan Publishers, 1994.

Shukr, A. G., *Political Alliances and Common Action in Egypt (1976–1993)*, Cairo: Kitab Al-Ahaly, 1994.

— (ed.), *Challenges of the Zionist Project and the Arab Confrontation*, Cairo: Arab Research Centre, 2001.

Syam, E., *Islamist Movement and NGOs in Egypt*, Unpublished Paper, Cairo: Arab Research Centre, 2000.

Thabet, A., *Cultural and Political Roles of the Non-Governmental Sector*, Cairo: Al-Ahram Centre for Political and Strategic Studies, 1999.

Information centres

Arab Research Centre, Cairo

Arab Association of Human Rights, Cairo

Egyptian Association of Human Rights, Cairo

Ibn Khaldoun Centre, Al Nida Al Jadid, Cairo

Encyclopedia of Arab NGOs – Al Ahram, Cairo

House for TV Services, Cairo

Arab NGO network for development, Beirut

Arab Branch of AWORD (Association of Women for Research and Development)

Association of Magrebian Women (Tunis)

Association des Femmes Démocrates (Tunis)

Arab Women Research Group (ARC, Cairo)

Index

Bled Siba (Morocco), 5, 27
Bosnia, 68
Boumédienne, Houari, 21, 22
Bourdieu, Pierre, 80
brain drain, 104
Bretton Woods institutions, 109–10, 117, 124
Bulgaria, 67, 68
businessmen's associations, 34

caliphate, 4, 29
Canada, 58, 97
Castells, Manuel, 76
Catalonia, modernization of, 65
Catholicism, 61, 64
Caucasus, 38
censorship, 25
Central and Eastern Europe, 108, 116
Centre Marocain de Conjoncture (CMC), 111, 112
Ceuta, 63
Chambers of Commerce, 17
Chevalier, Agnès, 86
children, subordination of, 1
China, 11, 13, 19, 21, 51, 52, 55, 56, 69, 79
Christian Democracy, 61
Christianity, 2, 6, 134
civil society, 27, 28, 36, 37, 83, 84, 86, 87, 93, 94, 95, 96, 123; mobilization of, 125; role of, 116
class struggle, 103
Cold War, 38, 67, 74, 78
colonialism, 22, 40, 57, 74, 77, 134
Common Agricultural Policy of EU, 105, 112
common markets, 44
communism, 9, 12, 13, 15, 21, 24, 53, 62; in Iraq, 20; in Syria, 20; in Third World, 17
Communist Party: Greece, 65; Palestine, 46, 47
communitarianism, 8–9
community associations, 31–8
comprador capitalism, 8, 9, 10, 14, 16, 70, 132

constitutions, 11
cooperative movements, 16
Copts, 34
corruption, 124
Croatia, 62, 67, 68
Crusades, 4
Cuba, blockade of, 41
Cyprus, 66
Cyprus, Turkish Republic of, 66

Dahmani, A., 110
Dalmatia, 62, 67
Dar El Harb, 4
Dar El Islam, 4
Darfur, 25
debt, 105–7, 112
decolonization, 59, 78
demobilization, 116
democracy, 22, 30, 71, 87, 95, 97, 137; in Arab world, 1, 2–3, 13, 14, 21, 23, 25, 27, 37, 38, 41, 42, 43; in Mediterranean zone, 83, 84, 89
Democratic Front for the Liberation of Palestine (DFLP), 46, 47
Democratic National Union (Egypt), 13
democratization, 123
demographic changes in Europe, 118
demographic transition, 107
denuclearization, 67
depoliticization, 18, 36, 44
despot, just, 3
development, 23, 40, 50, 69, 88, 93; projects, 19, 33; questioned, 50; women in, 34
development gap, 70
Dhofar, war in, 44
direct foreign investment, 113, 114, 116
diversity, ethnic, 27
drugs, from North Africa, 112
Druzes, 5

Eastern Europe, 69; Latin Americanization of, 53
ecology, in Arab world, 34

MERCOSUR, 104
Merton theory, 89
Mexico, 116; destruction of artisanal organization in, 112; effects of privatization in, 114; opening of economy of, 105
middle classes, 11, 16, 18, 24, 26, 27, 44, 46, 87, 95, 97, 98, 114, 123, 125, 132; loss of political interest, 116
Middle East common market project, 39, 57, 133
Middle East peace process, 91
migration and emigration, 15, 26, 94, 105; across Mediterranean, 82; and European Union, 81, 107; clandestine, problem of, 108; illegal, 94; in Arab world, 44, 132; in Mexico, 112 *see also* immigration
Mitidja, massacre of villagers, 22
Mittel-Europeanism, 61, 62
modernity, 2–3, 6, 7; opposition to, 7
modernization, 5, 10, 11, 12, 35, 40, 123
Mohamed Ali, 4, 10
monarchy: in Morocco, 26; parliamentary, 27
Morocco, 3, 5, 10, 25, 26–7, 29, 32, 34, 43, 63, 64, 85, 93, 102, 105, 109, 110, 115, 123, 132; debt of, 106, 112; elections in, 26; EU investment in, 113; export of labour, 107; migration from, 117; relation to free trade zone, 111–12; trade relations with Europe, 104
Multilateral Agreement on Investment (MAI), 112
multinational corporations, 113, 133, 137
Muslim Brotherhood, 12, 13, 16, 18, 20, 25, 46

Nafta, 81, 82, 102, 112, 117
nahda, 2–3, 10
Nasser, Gamal Abdel, 8, 12, 14–15, 18, 19

Nasserism, 11, 13, 15, 16, 17, 21, 131
nation-state, 76, 77, 80
National Democratic Alliance (Sudan), 25
National Democratic Party (Sudan), 23
national liberation, 18, 45
National Liberation Front (FLN) (Algeria), 21
national liberation movements, 21, 43
nationalism, 4, 8, 10, 11, 12, 13, 29, 30, 38, 39, 68, 95; Arab, 43; populist, 43–4
nationality, definition of, 23
natural resources, 52, 53
Nazism, 40
neo-imperialism, European, 72
neocolonialism, 59
neoliberalism, 28, 54, 57, 75, 76, 79, 80, 87, 95, 97, 102, 123, 124, 136
Netherlands, as donor country, 32
New Zealand, 58
non-alignment, 39
non-governmental organizations (NGOs), 25, 29, 30, 32–3, 36, 49, 85, 88, 95, 96, 98, 115, 116, 122; emergence of, 123–4
North American Free Trade Agreement (NAFTA), 79
North Atlantic Treaty Organization (NATO), 61, 63, 64, 65, 66, 67, 73, 134; involvement in Yugoslavia, 54
North–South relations, 72, 88, 94, 134
nuclear weapons, 72
El Numeiri, Gaafar, 24

oil industry, 32, 38
oil interests, 39, 40, 44, 52, 53, 58, 68, 70, 71, 100, 116, 132, 133
Operation Attila, 66
Organization of African Unity (OAU), 131
Orientalism, 6
Oslo accords, 41, 47, 48, 56, 122, 135, 136
Ottomans, 4, 5, 10, 29; Empire, 3, 11

Vatican, positions of, 61
Vietnam, 21; US defeat in, 55
Von Hayek, Friedrich, 30

Wafd, 8
Wahabism, 7, 10, 24, 25
waqf, suppression of, 29
Warsaw Pact, 67
Washington consensus, 97
water, management of, 90, 93
weapons of mass destruction, 50
welfare state, 102; spread of, 28
West Bank, 45
wilaya al faqih, 6, 25
women, 44; emancipation of, 3;
    literacy of, 103; marginalization
    of, 1; rights of, 4–5, 36

women's movements, 24
working class, 15, 22, 44, 94, 115;
    rights of, 34
World Bank, 32, 35, 37, 55, 75, 78, 87,
    95, 97, 103, 105, 111, 115, 136
World Trade Organization (WTO),
    78, 87, 95, 101, 136

Yalta Agreement, 65, 67
Yemen, 43, 44, 132
Youssofi, Abdel Rahman, 27
Yugoslavia, 65, 66–7, 68; blockade
    of, 41; EU stance on, 136–7;
    involvement of NATO in, 54; war
    in, 68, 69

Zionism, 41, 42, 45, 47, 48, 50, 133